UNVEILING THE FALL IN THE GARDEN OF EDEN: CLASSICAL AND MODERN INSIGHTS INTO THE TRUE MEANING OF ORIGINAL SIN

Upholding Baptismal Holiness and Overcoming Carnal Desires in a Postmodern Age

By

Christopher E. Ross

SANCTUS VIRTUE PUBLISHING

DEARBORN, MICHIGAN

© 2024 Sanctus Virtue Publishing, Dearborn, Michigan

All rights reserved

ISBN: 979-8-9916647-5-2

Library of Congress Catalog Card Number: 20-24924097

Printed in the United States of America

Contents

INTRODUCTION 1

CHAPTER 1:
THE TRANSFORMATION OF HUMAN NATURE AFTER ORIGINAL SIN 6
    THE EFFECTS OF ORIGINAL SIN: ALTERED HUMAN NATURE 10

CHAPTER 2:
THE SPIRITUAL AND PHYSICAL CONSEQUENCES OF ORIGINAL SIN 13
    THE ROLE OF THE SERPENT IN THE FALL OF MAN: SYMBOLISM, TEMPTATION, AND THE EMERGENCE OF A DISTORTED MORAL ORDER . 17
    ST. AUGUSTINE'S ANALYSIS OF ORIGINAL SIN: THE FALL OF ADAM AND EVE, THE INTRODUCTION OF SPIRITUAL AND PHYSICAL DEATH, AND THE NECESSITY OF BAPTISM 21
    THE CONSEQUENCES OF ORIGINAL SIN: THE DISRUPTION OF HARMONY, THE IMPOSITION OF MORTALITY, AND THE INTRODUCTION OF SUFFERING 22
    THE SYMBOLISM OF THE GARDEN AND THE SERPENT: DIVINE GOVERNANCE, THE LIMITS OF HUMAN FREEDOM, AND THE CONSEQUENCES OF DISOBEDIENCE 23
    THE CONSEQUENCES OF REJECTING DIVINE ORDER 25
    THE DENIAL OF CREATURELINESS AND ITS CONSEQUENCES 26
    THE RELATIONAL DAMAGE OF SIN AND ITS ORIGIN 28
    THE IMPACT OF THE SERPENT'S TEMPTATION: TRUST, DISOBEDIENCE, AND THE DISTORTION OF THE RELATIONSHIP WITH GOD 30

THE LEGACY OF ORIGINAL SIN: HUMANITY'S INHERITED WOUND AND THE PATH TO REDEMPTION 33

CHAPTER 3:

JESUS CHRIST'S SACRIFICE: THE ONLY REMEDY FOR ORIGINAL SIN 35

OVERCOMING ORIGINAL SIN: THE ROLE OF DIVINE GRACE AND THE SACRAMENTS...37

THE STRUGGLE AGAINST THE FLESH AND THE REDEMPTION THROUGH CHRIST 42

THE NECESSITY OF SACRIFICE FOR ATONEMENT: FROM OLD TESTAMENT RITUALS TO CHRIST'S ULTIMATE SACRIFICE......................44

THE DISTINCTION AND ELEVATION OF HUMAN NATURE THROUGH DIVINE GRACE...46

THE BONDAGE OF SIN AND THE REDEMPTION THROUGH CHRIST 47

THE ATONEMENT OF CHRIST: ANSELM'S SATISFACTION THEORY AND ITS IMPLICATIONS FOR ORIGINAL AND PERSONAL SIN 50

CHAPTER 4:
THEOLOGICAL BASIS FOR BAPTIZING INFANTS TO REMOVE ORIGINAL SIN 53

CHAPTER 5:
CONCUPISCENCE AFTER BAPTISM: STRUGGLE AND REWARD....................58

THE ONGOING NATURE OF CHRIST'S REDEMPTION: UNDERSTANDING THE ROLE OF SACRAMENTS, GRACE, AND RECONCILIATION IN CATHOLIC DOCTRINE..59

THE LIMITS OF SOLA FIDE: THE NECESSITY OF RECONCILIATION AND THE SACRAMENTAL ECONOMY IN ADDRESSING POST-BAPTISMAL SIN ..62

CHAPTER 6:

Overcoming the Carnal Nature 69
The Origin and Consequences of Carnal Nature 69
The Role of Divine Grace in Overcoming Concupiscence 70
The Sacred Purpose of Sexuality 71
Rejecting Impurity: Pornography, Masturbation, and
Lustful Behavior 74
The Sacrament of Reconciliation: Essential for Overcoming
Concupiscence 74
Guarding the Mind and Resisting Temptation 76
Restoring Baptismal Purity: Overcoming the Carnal Nature
through Grace and Virtue 77
The Devil's Tools in Tempting Us to Sexual Sin: The Dangers
of Seclusion and Sensory Manipulation 78
Cultivating a Life of Purity 79
Choosing Holiness Over Compromise: A Call to Purity in
Relationships 80
Practical Steps for Maintaining Purity and Resisting
Temptation 81

CONCLUSION 84

BIBLIOGRAPHY 88

EXPLORE MORE FROM SANCTUS VIRTUE PUBLISHING 90

Introduction

Discover the profound depth of Catholic teaching on original sin and salvation in this illuminating treatise, where the timeless struggle of concupiscence is met with the transformative power of the sacraments. Explore how baptism restores us to a state of grace yet reveals the necessity of ongoing vigilance and reconciliation in the face of post-baptismal sin. Delve into the rich theological contrasts between Catholic and Protestant views on salvation and uncover why the sacrament of reconciliation is not just a ritual but a vital means of grace that upholds divine justice and mercy. This treatise offers a compelling examination of how the Church's sacramental economy provides the essential tools for spiritual growth and redemption, making it a must-read for anyone seeking a deeper understanding of faith and forgiveness.

In my discussion of the classical doctrine of original sin, I will adhere strictly to the guidelines established by the Council of Trent to ensure a faithful and orthodox presentation of the topic. The Council of Trent provides a clear framework for understanding original sin, emphasizing its transmission from Adam and Eve, its impact on human nature, and the necessity of baptism for its removal. By grounding my exploration in the proofs and teachings affirmed by Trent, I will navigate the complexities of this doctrine while avoiding deviations into heretical interpretations. This approach will ensure that the discussion remains aligned with the Church's magisterial teachings and maintains doctrinal integrity throughout.

The upcoming chapter, "The Transformation of Human Nature After Original Sin," delves into the profound changes that occurred in humanity following the transgression of Adam and Eve. Drawing from authoritative Catholic sources such as the Council of Trent and the writings of St. Robert Bellarmine, it elucidates the theological ramifications of original sin. Initially endowed with divine gifts and in a state of original holiness and justice, this first act of disobedience irrevocably altered humanity's nature. This transformation resulted in the loss of original righteousness, subjection to sin and death, and the inheritance of a corrupted nature by all subsequent generations. Understanding this doctrinal foundation is crucial for comprehending the necessity of Christ's redemptive work and the continuing struggle against moral failings in human life. Through Christ's passion and resurrection, the pathway to restoration and divine grace is opened, highlighting the profound significance of the sacrament of baptism and the hope of ultimate redemption.

The upcoming passage "The Effects of Original Sin: Altered Human Nature" explores the profound consequences of Adam and Eve's disobedience, which fundamentally transformed human nature from its original state of justice and holiness to one marked by injustice and unholiness. This alteration, known as concupiscence, refers to a strong inclination toward sin and an involuntary attraction to pleasure that persists even after baptism. This intrinsic weakness makes humans susceptible to coveting earthly goods and pursuing self-centered ends, often in conflict with reason and spiritual goals. Concupiscence, a central concept in understanding human frailty, highlights the inner struggle against sinful desires and the necessity of divine grace for moral and spiritual resilience. Through this examination, the passage underscores the pervasive impact of original sin on humanity's moral and spiritual life, necessitating continual resistance and the pursuit of grace to overcome these inherent inclinations.

The doctrine of original sin is central to Christian theology, particularly in understanding the profound impact of Adam and Eve's transgression on humanity. According to the Council of Trent, Adam's sin did not merely affect him alone but had devastating consequences for all his descendants. This passage explores the dual nature of these consequences—spiritual and physical—emphasizing that through Adam's disobedience, sin entered the world, resulting in both spiritual death (separation from God's grace) and physical death (the end of earthly life). This inherited sin, termed original sin, marks every human being from conception, necessitating divine intervention and the sacrament of baptism for spiritual restoration. The passage further delves into the relational and existential disruptions caused by original sin, highlighting how it altered human nature, strained relationships, and introduced suffering and mortality into the human experience. Through this exploration, the passage underscores the depth of humanity's fall and the enduring need for reconciliation with God.

The profound implications of original sin and the redemptive sacrifice of Jesus Christ are central to Christian theology and the understanding of human salvation. The passage from the Council of Trent highlights the crucial doctrine that Jesus Christ's sacrifice is the sole remedy for the sin inherited from Adam. It asserts that no human effort or alternative remedy can remove the stain of original sin, which affects every individual. The Council's declaration underscores the necessity of Christ's atoning work, which not only reconciles humanity with God but also reaffirms the essential role of baptism in applying the merits of Christ's sacrifice. This introduction delves into the theological significance of Jesus Christ's sacrifice, exploring how it addresses the consequences of original sin and restores the broken communion between humanity and God. It also considers the implications of divine grace, sacramental rites, and the ongoing need for Christ's redemptive work in the face of human weakness and sin.

The question whether infants should be baptized has been a point of theological debate throughout Christian history. According to the Council of Trent, the necessity of infant baptism is rooted in the belief that all humanity inherits original sin from Adam, regardless of the parents' baptized status. This passage affirms that baptism is essential for infants to cleanse them of the original sin that they inherit from birth, ensuring their entry into the Kingdom of Heaven. Through baptism, even those who have not committed personal sin are purified from the inherent defect of original sin. As highlighted by early Church teachings and analogies, this sacrament is a fundamental means of grace, pivotal for restoring the soul to a state of sanctifying grace and reconciling it with God.

The Catholic understanding of salvation and sin involves a nuanced view of concupiscence and the ongoing role of Christ's redemptive work. Following baptism, while the guilt of original sin is removed and one is restored to a state of grace, some of the inclination to sin—concupiscence—remains. This inclination, though not considered actual sin, presents a continual struggle that requires vigilant resistance through the grace provided by Christ. The Catholic Church asserts that the sacraments, including reconciliation, are essential for addressing personal sin committed after baptism. This perspective contrasts sharply with the Protestant belief in sola fide, which posits that faith alone is sufficient for salvation and often disregards the need for formal reconciliation and the role of the sacraments in maintaining one's spiritual well-being. Understanding this dynamic, highlights the importance of the sacramental economy in Catholic doctrine and underscores the ongoing necessity of grace and repentance in the Christian life.

Chapter 1:
THE TRANSFORMATION OF HUMAN NATURE AFTER ORIGINAL SIN

> *"If anyone does not confess that the first man, Adam, when he transgressed the commandment of God in paradise, immediately lost the holiness and justice in which he had been constituted, and through the offense of that prevarication incurred the wrath and indignation of God, and thus death with which God had previously threatened him, and together with death, captivity under his power who thenceforth had the empire of death, that is to say, the devil, and that the entire Adam through the offense of prevarication was changed in body and soul for the worse, let him be anathema." (Council of Trent, Session 5, "Decree on Original Sin," Canon 1, in The Canons and Decrees of the Council of Trent, trans. H.J. Schroeder [Rockford: Tan Books and Publishers, 1978], 21).*[1]

According to St. Robert Bellarmine in his Doctrina Christiana, "Original Sin is that sin which we are born with because it descends to us from our first parent in succession. For that reason, it must be noted that when God made the first man and woman, who He called Adam and Eve, He bestowed upon them seven gifts. The first was the grace that made them just and friends of God and His adopted sons. Second, He bestowed upon them great knowledge to know, do

---

[1] Council of Trent, Session 5, "Decree on Original Sin," Canon 1, in The Canons and Decrees of the Council of Trent, trans. H.J. Schroeder, (Rockford: Tan Books and Publishers, 1978), 21)

good, and turn away from evil. Third, He allotted such obedience to them that the flesh would obey the spirit and would not rebel against reason for the sake of illicit desires. Fourthly, He gave the greatest alacrity and facility to do good and turn away from evil, and He prescribed none but that one and easy command. Fifthly, He made them free from every vexation and fear because the earth itself produced sufficient fruits for the propagation of human life of its own will and unplowed, nor was there anything that could harm man. Sixthly, he made them immortal so that they could never die if they were not contaminated with sin. Seventhly, He willed after some time to transfer them to Heaven, to the glorious and eternal life that the angels enjoyed.

But the devil deceived the first man and woman, and they did not observe that command and so sinned against God that they lost these seven gifts. Moreover, since God had conferred these gifts upon them not only for their own person but their posterity, when our parents lost them, they not only lost them for themselves but for us. They not only made themselves partakers of sin but also of every misery, in the same way as they were previously partakers of grace and the goods, which they possessed so long as they would not sin. Therefore, original sin is enmity with God and a loss of divine grace; we are born with this loss. It is from this sin that all ignorance proceeds, just as wicked inclination, the difficulty to do good and the ease to do evil, the punishment and work of providing things necessary for life, as well as fear and the dangers set about us, the certain death of the body and the eternal death of hell if, before the moment of our death, we will not be freed from sin and restored to grace."[2]

Before Original Sin, i.e., Adam and Eve's fall, man was in a state of original holiness and justice; they were sharers in divine life because God, being all good, did not create man to be evil or have the inclination to do evil. This original justice and holiness meant that man's mind was naturally virtuous, endowed with a spiritual mind that adhered to God, along with a strong sense of original chastity, temperance, and charity.[3] They were in a state of divine life, where harmony and transparency were central to existence, and if man continued to reside in this divine intimacy, man would not suffer nor die.

When Adam and Eve ate from the Tree of the Knowledge of Good and Evil, by disobeying God's commandment, Adam and Eve lost this sense of charity and were found to be evil.[4] Because man listened to the prince of vices and committed sin, man lost the gifts of original justice and holiness (spiritual mind, temperance, charity, and chastity). Hence, human nature from that point on, the flesh becomes corrupted and altered, and any child that came forth after the fall became tainted with original sin, meaning all people are born with the altered form of human nature.

---

[2] Bellarmine, Robert, et al. Doctrina Christiana: The Timeless Catechism of St. Robert Bellarmine. Lulu.com, 28 Sept. 2016, pg. 217-218

[3] Peter Lombard, Sentences, Volume 2, Distinction XXIX, Chapter 2, trans. Guilio Silano, (Toronto: Pontifical Institute of Mediaeval Studies, 2007), 143.

[4] Ibid

If Adam and Eve had preserved their original justice and holiness, then those born of them would also be in the state of original justice and holiness.[5] Before they committed original sin, they were strong and uncorrupted. They had the power to maintain original justice and holiness forever without difficulty, but after they committed original sin, their bodies became like brute animals subject to carnal desires and corruption; the human soul became tainted by the passions of the flesh and lost the benefits it once had.[6] Because the wholeness of human nature was in them, it worked to weaken human nature in its entirety.[7]

Understanding original sin is paramount to understanding the role of Jesus Christ in terms of redemption, which provides clear insight into the human condition. It provides a clear insight into how man is prone to error and moral failings and why there is a need for divine intervention and moral restoration. Because of original sin, even though man has free will, the devil here acquired a certain power and domination over man due to his wounded nature and inclination toward evil, which continues to give rise to errors in the most important facets of life, such as politics, social issues, education, and most important of all morality.[8]

---

[5] Anselm (saint). Why God Became Man. Magi Publications, 1969, pg. 171

[6] Ibid

[7] Ibid

[8] Catholic Church. (2019). Catechism of the Catholic Church. Vatican City, Libreria Editrice Vaticana; Washington, D.C, para. 407, pg. 103

God made for humanity a way to satisfy original sin through the remedy and passion of our Lord Jesus Christ.[9] Jesus Christ, acting as both God and man, frees us from original sin through His death and resurrection, and the fruits of this remedy are applied to us by Holy Baptism.[10] Although we will not be restored all these gifts at once, what will be restored after baptism is the most principal one: the grace of making us just and friends of God, as well as sons of God, not in substance, but heirs to His Heavenly Kingdom; the remaining gifts will be given to us in the next life, given that we lived this life well in accordance with the standards imposed to us by God.[11]

THE EFFECTS OF ORIGINAL SIN: ALTERED HUMAN NATURE

After Adam and Eve disobeyed God, this sin was so grievous that it literally altered human nature from original justice and holiness to an altered nature of injustice and unholiness. The effect of the fall altered human nature, giving human nature a strong inclination toward sin or a strong incentive to sin, meaning man became subjugated to the pleasures of his or her senses, which caused man to inordinately covet earthly goods and self-assertion that were contrary to spiritual ends and reason[12]; this is what is called concupiscence, the concept meaning in short, a weakness in

---

[9] Bellarmine, Robert, et al. Doctrina Christiana: The Timeless Catechism of St. Robert Bellarmine. Lulu.com, 28 Sept. 2016, pg. 219

[10] Ibid

[11] Bellarmine, Robert, et al. Doctrina Christiana: The Timeless Catechism of St. Robert Bellarmine. Lulu.com, 28 Sept. 2016, pg. 219

[12] University of Notre Dame McGrath Institute for Church Life. (n.d.). Foundations of Catholic Belief. Unit 4: Salvation in Jesus Christ, Section "Sin and Its Effects" (CCC, 355-421 and 2331-2347). Retrieved from mcgrath.nd.edu.

human nature, an attraction to pleasure, that gives it a tendency or inclination toward sin, a type of involuntary sexual desire and/arousal, or an inclination toward sinful lust.[13] The word comes from the Latin word "concupiscentia," which means "strong desire" or "lust." It is often described as a strong and intense desire or a human inclination toward something considered wrong or sinful, an inclination to sin, even after baptism. It often takes form toward physical pleasures, such as food, drink, and sexual activity, and there is intellectual concupiscence, meaning an inclination for the pursuit of knowledge that is self-centered or unethical, such as knowledge of the occult, using knowledge to manipulate, adopting moral relativism, rationalizing unethical behaviors, etc.

This weakness in human nature must be resisted and is the primary means the devil uses against man to call man to do evil; it is a type of inner tyranny over man's soul. To make the enemy defenseless, man must accept grace and not obey the evil concupiscence in the soul; the very incentive to sin is concupiscence.[14] This altered and fallen sense of human nature as a consequence of Adam, the first human being to disobey God in the Garden of Eden, is a condition that affects all human beings, compelling human beings and making them inclined to sin. This inherited concupiscence causes man to be attracted to sin, often into morally wrong pleasures; it's the very inclination

---

[13] Peter Lombard, Sentences, Volume 2, Distinction XXX, Chapter 8, trans. Guilio Silano, (Toronto: Pontifical Institute of Mediaeval Studies, 2007), 149.

[14] Ibid

to commit sinful acts. It is a type of internal struggle within human beings where their bodily desires conflict with their better judgment, conscience, moral values, and rational will.

According to Romans 7:23,*But I see another law in my members, warring against the law of my mind, and bringing me into captivity to the law of sin which is in my members.*[15] This internal struggle and inclination toward sin makes it difficult for mankind to resist sinful desires. It being tyrannical over the human soul means that this inner tendency toward sin can dominate and control human behavior; it inclines one to act as opposed to the spirit, which seeks to follow God's law. According to Saint Augustine, man must overcome the tyrant of concupiscence, must turn away and resist sinful desires, and seek moral and spiritual strength. Following this inclination toward sin creates the very entry point toward evil influences. This inherited concupiscence is in human beings from Adam the first human being, and it's an internal struggle in mankind between bodily desires and/or appetites that goes against spiritual aspirations and brings man into need for grace, self-discipline, and moral vigilance. Because Adam was mankind's first parent, he was the father of a generation, and all those in the generation originated in him; this sin and/or fallen nature was transmitted to all his descendants; this is why it is called original.[16]

---

[15] Video autem aliam legem in membris meis repugnantem legi mentis meae, et captivantem me in lege peccati, quae est in membris meis.

[16] Thomas Aquinas. Summa Theologiae: Prima Secundae Partis, Q. 81, Art. 1. Translated by the Fathers of the English Dominican Province, Aquinas Institute, Green Bay, WI, pg. 113

Chapter 2:

THE SPIRITUAL AND PHYSICAL CONSEQUENCES OF ORIGINAL SIN

"If anyone asserts that the transgression of Adam injured him alone and not his posterity, and that the holiness and justice which he received from God, which he lost, he lost for himself alone and not for us also; or that he, being defiled by the sin of disobedience, has transfused only death and the pains of the body into the whole human race, but not sin also, which is the death of the soul, let him be anathema, since he contradicts the Apostle who says: By one man sin entered into the world and by sin death; and so death passed upon all men, in whom all have sinned." Council of Trent, Session 5, "Decree on Original Sin," Canon 2, in The Canons and Decrees of the Council of Trent, trans. H.J. Schroeder, (Rockford: Tan Books and Publishers, 1978), 21-22) 17

Once Adam committed original sin, human nature was altered. This alteration, namely the vice of concupiscence, entered Adam's posterity, meaning we all became sharers in that stain of sin.[18] Adam corrupted himself, and every soul that came from his posterity was corrupted, thus staining all of us with original sin, which means that we all sinned.[19] As the Apostle says: *By one man sin entered*

---

[17] Council of Trent, Session 5, "Decree on Original Sin," Canon 2, in The Canons and Decrees of the Council of Trent, trans. H.J. Schroeder, (Rockford: Tan Books and Publishers, 1978), 21-22

[18] Peter Lombard, Sentences, Volume 2, Distinction XXX, Chapter 10, trans. Guilio Silano, (Toronto: Pontifical Institute of Mediaeval Studies, 2007), 150.

[19] Ibid

into the world and by sin death; and so death passed upon all men, in whom all have sinned (Romans 5:12). This means we are all born sinners because we are conceived in concupiscence, which was issued from Adam through his disobedience which passed unto all his posterity.[20] This one man's sin, which entered into the world, is referred to as original sin.[21]

The truth of the matter is that if the first men had not committed original sin, mankind would not have experienced any type of death, whether physical or spiritual, meaning spiritual death, moral and spiritual alienation from God, and physical death, meaning the end of earthly existence as we know it.[22] Because Adam and Eve committed original sin, they were punished with death, and because of this, their offspring were punished with death.[23] God warned Adam:*in the day ye eat of it ye shall die the death*, meaning that if man chose to desert God in disobedience, God would desert man in perfect justice.[24]

When they committed the sin, whether it was actually eating fruit from a tree or whether it had a symbolic meaning, they felt shame and covered this shame and hid it from God. Here, they experienced the first death, which was spiritual death, where God forsakes the soul, and because the soul also forsook the body, the body then became corrupted and decayed

---

[20] Peter Lombard, Sentences, Volume 2, Distinction XXX, Chapter 12, trans. Guilio Silano, (Toronto: Pontifical Institute of Mediaeval Studies, 2007), 151.

[21] Peter Lombard, Sentences, Volume 2, Distinction XXX, Chapter 12, trans. Guilio Silano, (Toronto: Pontifical Institute of Mediaeval Studies, 2007), 151.

[22] Of Hippo, Augustine,. City of God. Translated by Marcus Dods, Digireads.com Publishing, 2017, pg. 351

[23] Ibid

[24] Ibid, pg. 359

with age, and earthly death was also pronounced as part of man's sentence; *Earth thou art, and unto earth shall thou return.*[25] Even though Adam's posterity did not commit original sin personally, as a consequence, all of Adam's posterity suffered the consequences of having flesh inclined to sin, and all were made mortal because of the eating of the fruit.[26]

Whether the fruit was actual fruit or symbolic, it is important to note, according to the Church Fathers: 1). disobedience, 2). seeking moral autonomy outside of God, 3). mistrust in God, 4). turning away from divine wisdom, and 5). spiritual failing and pride are the core issues associated with it, not so much in the actual eating of the fruit or whether this symbolically represented a type of grievous sin. After they ate from the tree, they were banished from paradise; it is explained that God clothed them with coats of skin. According to Gregory of Nazianzus, this means flesh, flesh being both mortal and rebellious.[27] Death was imposed as a punishment; even though it seems like a punishment, it is a type of mercy because death prevents sin from perpetuating itself.[28]

Being banished from paradise and because being a being capable of change due to not being self-sustaining as God is, according to St. Augustine, means when Adam and Eve chose to do what the Supreme Truth forbade, man became banished

---

[25] Of Hippo, Augustine,. City of God. Translated by Marcus Dods, Digireads.com Publishing, 2017, pg. 359

[26] Henri Rondet, Original Sin: The Patristic and Theological Background. Saint Pauls/Alba House, 1 Jan. 1972, pg. 107

[27] Ibid, pg. 99

[28] Ibid

from paradise (a state of eternal communion with God) into the temporal world (physical and mortal existence), going from eternity to time, from riches to poverty, from strength and stability to weakness and instability. The tree planted was not something evil; it was the breach of the prohibition that was meddled with, and that was the source of the evil.[29] When they ate from the tree, humans gained an awareness of good and evil. This knowledge came through experience of sin and its consequences.[30] Once this happened, the soul became trapped in its own sin that was now in need of atonement because now the soul recognizes the gravity of its disobedience and the true nature of sin through experience; thus, it learns the difference between God's commandment and the sin it has committed. Through the consequences of sin, the soul learns the true nature of sin and obedience; from the results of sin, he begins to understand the need for atonement and how important it is to stand in obedience rather than disobedience.[31]

---

[29] Ibid. 114

[30] Ibid

[31] Henri Rondet, Original Sin: The Patristic and Theological Background. Saint Pauls/Alba House, 1 Jan. 1972, pg. 114

THE ROLE OF THE SERPENT IN THE FALL OF MAN: SYMBOLISM, TEMPTATION, AND THE EMERGENCE OF A DISTORTED MORAL ORDER

The serpent that tempted Adam and Eve played a crucial role in man's moral and spiritual downfall. The serpent, more than likely a symbolic representation of evil or evil inspiration, not an actual snake, persuaded Adam and Eve to eat from the forbidden tree. By them eating from it, it was not merely a transgression of a divine command, but a fundamental rejection of God's established moral order. The serpent's cunning deception persuaded man to have doubt and skepticism in God's wisdom and goodness, and the serpent persuaded man that if they ate of the tree, they would be "like gods" (Genesis 3:5), meaning they would be able to define good and evil based upon their own judgment without and over divine authority; here, instead of relying on God for the true sense of good and evil, they sought to define good and evil upon their own terms; thus making up their own moral system.

Here, Adam and Eve chose to listen to the serpent and prioritize their own understanding over God's commandments. They chose to rebel against divine authority and attempted to establish their own moral system based upon human desires and inclinations rather than divine truth and God's established moral system. This act of rebellion fractured their perfect communion with God and resulted in spiritual death, a separation from God's grace, and a distortion of human nature. This very corruption brought the imposition of spiritual and physical death. Because of original sin, man found himself drawn to that which is wrong and evil, being created by the All-

Good Creator, from which this inclination of evil cannot come. The relationship between God and man became altered in the negative, and the right order within man was broken, breaking the harmony between God, man, creatures, and creation.[32]

As far as the serpent goes, it may have been an actual snake or a symbolic representation of the devil and his evil, or the serpent was an instrument of the devil. God did not create evil or the devil; He created angels and gave them certain tasks and missions, such as being messengers, etc.[33] Angels are and were created spirits as humans are; they are still creatures, and because they are creatures, they are limited, while God is unlimited. Some of them fell because of pride, the desire to be like God, and freely choosing to disobey God. Because of the fall, some of them began to hate all that God loves, reflecting their opposition to God's will and having envy and jealousy toward humans and God's creation.

Being spiritual beings' repentance is not accepted, just as it will not be accepted from us after death. *By the envy of the Devil, death entered the World* (Wisdom 2:24). The devil originally was an angel that God created, and he became evil by his own doing and free choice.[34] Because of the hate and works of the devil, God sent His only Son into the world to destroy the works of the devil.[35] Through some wisdom we may not fully

---

[32] Catholic Church. (2019). Catechism of the Catholic Church. Vatican City, Libreria Editrice Vaticana; Washington, D.C, para. 401, pg. 101

[33] Ibid, para. 355-391, pg. 91-100

[34] Ibid

[35] Ibid

understand, Satan is allowed to exist and act through Divine Providence. Even though the devil acts diabolically, because God is all good, everything ultimately works for the good of those who love God (Romans 8:28).[36]

According to St. Basil the Great, physical evil, such as diseases and natural disasters, does not arise from a moral choice, yet moral evil originates in misusing human free will. It does not come from God. Both humans and angels have the ability to choose moral evil by going against God's will. Original sin originated with the devil, but the devil was not made a devil; he is a fallen angel.[37] The reason for his fall was his jealousy of man's happiness, which ultimately brought about his fall. When the devil led Adam and Eve astray into original sin, his motives were that of pride and envy against us, and even to this day, he still remains prideful and envious toward humanity.

The consequences of the misuse of our created freedom have affected the entire world.[38] God is not the author of evil; evil stems from sin, and sin began in the intellectual and spiritual world first. During the time when Angels were receiving their ministries and/or duties or posts, one of them was given the office of governing the earth in the way God would instruct Angels to govern the earth. When God created

---

[36] Catholic Church. (2019). Catechism of the Catholic Church. Vatican City, Libreria Editrice Vaticana; Washington, D.C, para. 355-391, pg. 91-100

[37] Henri Rondet, Original Sin: The Patristic and Theological Background. Saint Pauls/Alba House, 1 Jan. 1972, pg. 92

[38] Henri Rondet, Original Sin: The Patristic and Theological Background. Saint Pauls/Alba House, 1 Jan. 1972, pg. 92

man, because of the way that God favored man, this particular angel became jealous, and because of this jealousy and envy, he cunningly induced man to disobey God and commit sin.[39] Sin works to decay the integrity of the spirit, darkens the intellect, and hardens the will; us being both spiritual and material beings, sins work to make us overly focused on the material and sensual objects world by averting us from spiritual growth and divine connection; thus leading to moral, spiritual, and intellectual degradation.[40]

---

[39] pg. 97

[40] Ibid

ST. AUGUSTINE'S ANALYSIS OF ORIGINAL SIN: THE FALL OF ADAM AND EVE, THE INTRODUCTION OF SPIRITUAL AND PHYSICAL DEATH, AND THE NECESSITY OF BAPTISM

In St. Augustine's "City of God," the notion of crafting our own moral system in opposition to God's divine order is intricately tied to the concept of original sin. Augustine argues that Adam and Eve's fall stemmed from their decision to pursue their own wisdom and moral judgment, rejecting the divine guidance provided by God. This act of disobedience, rooted in a desire for autonomy and self-determination, introduced spiritual death into the human experience. By choosing to define good and evil apart from God, they not only severed their relationship with the divine but also ushered in spiritual alienation for all humanity. This spiritual death, characterized by a profound separation from God's grace, is the root cause of human suffering and moral confusion.

Consequently, physical death entered the world as a direct consequence of this original sin, marking the transition from an intended eternal communion with God to a finite and mortal existence. Thus, Augustine underscores that the fall of Adam and Eve not only corrupted our moral compass but also imposed the dual punishment of spiritual and physical death, illustrating the profound impact of deviating from God's sovereign will. Whether Adam and Eve ate fruit or rather it represented some act of disobedience, it was a grievous sin that altered human nature negatively. This alteration affected all of Adam's posterity, and because of this sin, mankind became subject to physical and spiritual death (death of the soul & inclination toward evil).[41] Because of this, the Church even baptizes infants who have not committed personal sin because they are still subject to original sin because it is the flesh that is corrupted.

THE CONSEQUENCES OF ORIGINAL SIN: THE DISRUPTION OF HARMONY, THE IMPOSITION OF MORTALITY, AND THE INTRODUCTION OF SUFFERING

Before the fall, Adam and Eve enjoyed a state of original justice, characterized by perfect harmony and transparency with God, each other, and all of creation. Their original sin disrupted this harmony, leading to a profound change in their relationships. After their act of disobedience, they became aware of their nakedness and felt shame. This loss of innocence made them ashamed of their vulnerability, prompting them to hide and obscure their transparency. Their once harmonious relationships were replaced by disharmony, marked by suspicion, blame, and conflict. The unity, trust, and transparency that had previously defined their interactions gave way to discord and manipulation. Here, as a punishment for original sin, the union or partnership between man and woman became the subject of various tensions, filled with lust and domination in place of harmony and transparency; here, the harmony that once existed was now broken.[42]

---

[41] Of Hippo, Augustine,. City of God. Translated by Marcus Dods, Digireads.com Publishing, 2017, pg. 389

[42] Catholic Church. (2019). Catechism of the Catholic Church. Vatican City, Libreria Editrice Vaticana; Washington, D.C, para. 400, pg. 100-101

Because of original sin, as mercy, we were punished with mortality to transition into an afterlife because physical death was not part of God's original plan and only became a reality due to the fall. It is a mercy because God would not want man to live in eternity in the current fallen world order. The further punishments for original sin, the act and making up a moral order separate from the divine, women must experience childbirth pains (Genesis 3:16), and men have to toil and struggle for work to make a living (Genesis 3:17-19). Suffering came into existence because of sin. They were expelled from the Garden, meaning they were removed from paradise and the divine intimacy they once had with God. Their relationship with God was broken, and they lost their original state of holiness and justice.

THE SYMBOLISM OF THE GARDEN AND THE SERPENT: DIVINE GOVERNANCE, THE LIMITS OF HUMAN FREEDOM, AND THE CONSEQUENCES OF DISOBEDIENCE

The garden here is a symbolic representation of the world, as it provides us nourishment, shelter, and sustenance, and it came into being by the will of the Creator.[43] The right understanding is that God and His creation are intermixed, and the problem happens when human beings seek to detach it from God's governance, claiming it as their own property, exploiting it for their own selfish ends, instead of looking it as a

---

[43] Benedict, Pope. In the Beginning--: A Catholic Understanding of the Story of Creation and the Fall. Grand Rapids, Mich., W.B. Eerdmans Pub. Co, 1995, pg. 64

gift, respecting God's governance and using it what God intended it for.[44]

When it comes to the serpent, it is symbolic of the devil. Also, within the context at the time, the serpent represented pagan eastern fertility cults that constantly tempted Israel to leave the covenant and plunge into delirium and ecstasy of the once current world order for a few moments, being freed from divine power.[45] The serpent, being cunning, tempted Adam not to disbelieve in God. The serpent made a reasonable request, yet the diabolical nature of his request lured man from trust to mistrust. He sowed doubt about God's Divine Order and Governance, meaning doubt about God's covenant with man, doubt about the community of faith, prayer, and God's commandments.[46] Instead of subjugating oneself to the Creator and His governance, the serpent made freedom from it look attractive. He made subjugating oneself to the Divine Order look like something oppressive, making it appear as if the Divine Order is robbing people of their freedom and the most precious things in this life.[47]

---

[44] Ibid, pg. 64-65

[45] ibid

[46] Benedict, Pope. In the Beginning--: A Catholic Understanding of the Story of Creation and the Fall. Grand Rapids, Mich., W.B. Eerdmans Pub. Co, 1995, pg. 66

[47] Ibid

THE CONSEQUENCES OF REJECTING DIVINE ORDER

Here, they started to see that God's moral order was a type of limitation on their existence. Here, they sought to be freed from God's moral order, looking at it as a limitation instead of a Divine Gift.[48] The Tree of Knowledge of Good and Evil symbolizes the inherent limitations that human beings, being creatures of God, must respect; it represents boundaries set by God that humans must acknowledge to maintain a proper relationship with God. The Tree of the Knowledge of Good and Evil is figurative, not biological, in the sense it represents the authority of determining good and evil, which solely belong to God, and the Tree of Life represents God being the vine and we being the branches; they both being represented as trees is because we draw life, shelter, and fruit from trees.[49]

When human beings eat from the Tree of the Knowledge of Good and Evil, it symbolically means through pride, taking on the authority to do what humans believe to be good in their own eyes independently from God, disregarding what God determines is good and evil; when they do this, it ultimately leads to corrupted human nature, broken relationships, violence, and death, even though this tree symbolically looks attractive to human beings.[50] It is not inherently bad to have knowledge of good and evil. As long as it comes from a relationship with God and obedience to His Will, it becomes

---

[48] Ibid

[49] Day 55: The Fall of the Angels — The Catechism in a Year (with Fr. Mike Schmitz) https://www.youtube.com/watch?v=QiJL024zpmc

[50] Ibid

bad when it is acquired through disobedience and defiance. When human beings did this in the beginning, they were exiled from paradise.[51] Human beings are endowed with freedom but must use this freedom in harmony with God's established moral order. When they use their freedom outside God's moral order and begin to create their own moral order, this is where the problem starts.

THE DENIAL OF CREATURELINESS AND ITS CONSEQUENCES

By man subjugating himself to God's covenant and moral order, man is accepting that he is a creature of God, and he is affirming his creatureliness.[52] When man listened to the serpent and chose to disobey God, creating his own moral order, he committed sin, and at the heart of sin lies their denial of their own creatureliness by refusing to accept the limitations and standards that make up being a creature of God.[53]

Here, man no longer sought to be a creature of God, being dependent and subject to a standard created by God; they saw this subjugation as a type of slavery and sought freedom from it, and sought to be God by denying their creatureliness and imposing their own moral order.[54] When they did this, everything became thrown into disarray. Once this happened, man's relationships to God, others, to self, and creation became

---

[51] Ibid

[52] Benedict, Pope. In the Beginning--: A Catholic Understanding of the Story of Creation and the Fall. Grand Rapids, Mich., W.B. Eerdmans Pub. Co, 1995, pg. 70

[53] Ibid

[54] Ibid

altered in such a way that instead of harmony and transparency, it became one of destruction and exploitation.[55]

The sinful, the ones who seek to free themselves from their creatureliness, are, in fact, denying the highest love and denying the truth about themselves, wanting to free themselves. In doing so, they actually deny ultimate truth and love.[56] The problem is that they don't become gods as the serpent claimed. Still, with false, distorted versions of gods, people become enslaved to these false gods and their false moral systems, ultimately leading to humanity's downfall.[57]

Eating from the forbidden tree means that human beings deny the limitations set upon them by God's moral order of good and evil, which are the foundations and standards of creation as we know it. They end up denying the truth; by denying this truth, man begins to live in untruth and unreality, and their lives become a simple appearance that is surrounded by untruths and unlife, which causes spiritual and physical death.[58]

---

[55] Benedict, Pope. In the Beginning--: A Catholic Understanding of the Story of Creation and the Fall. Grand Rapids, Mich., W.B. Eerdmans Pub. Co, 1995, pg. 70

[56] Benedict, Pope. In the Beginning--: A Catholic Understanding of the Story of Creation and the Fall. Grand Rapids, Mich., W.B. Eerdmans Pub. Co, 1995, pg. 70-71

[57] Ibid, pg. 71

[58] Ibid

THE RELATIONAL DAMAGE OF SIN AND ITS ORIGIN

The truth of the matter is that sin begets sin, and because sin begets sin, the history of sin becomes interlinked.[59] Human beings are not complete individuals; they are relational by nature. We are born into a world from the womb of our mothers, our families raise us, and we become interlinked with each other. Sin is damaging to the nature of our relationality; it is a type of rejection of our natural relationality in the pursuit of man wanting to be a god.[60] Sin is about the loss, damage, and disturbance of relationships in themselves; it negatively alters the world and thus damages it.[61] Original sin creates massive relational damage, and a human being comes into the relationally damaged world.[62]

No matter what humans do, because the world is stained by sin, sin actively seeks out individuals as a persistent force that, no matter what humans do, they have to surrender or succumb to, meaning humans are forced to succumb to a sin-damaged world. There exists a human weakness and a constant struggle against moral failings.[63]

The true nature of sin is not simply an act but the corruption that comes before the act takes place. According to St Augustine, "for the evil act had never been done had not an evil

---

[59] Ibid, pg. 72
[60] Ibid, pg. 72-73
[61] Ibid, pg. 73
[62] Ibid
[63] Ibid

will preceded it,"[64] and the origin of evil will is pride, and pride starts with a desire for exultation that one does not truly deserve.[65] As said before, the true self of humanity is living as a creature of God subject to His moral order. Pride here was the desire to be more than a creature of God. When man aspired to be self-sufficient because of pride, man fell away from the very source of his existence: creatureliness.

Pride goeth before destruction, when the serpent said *Ye shall be as Gods,* the very origin of wanting to be a God is the seeking of undeserved exultation, and sin is what disturbs relationality between that which exists and the desire to live according to one's own moral order, to live according to oneself is another aspect of sin. Here, before Adam and Eve committed the act of original sin, the serpent beguiled them and coaxed them into the lust of undue exultation, i.e., pride, and the myth of self-sufficiency to live according to one's own self and one's own moral order, once the human will was corrupted then the evil act of disobedience occurred; as St. Augustine said: "for the evil act had never been done had not an evil will preceded it."

---

[64] Of Hippo, Augustine,. City of God. Translated by Marcus Dods, Digireads.com Publishing, 2017, pg. 389
[65] Ibid

THE IMPACT OF THE SERPENT'S TEMPTATION: TRUST, DISOBEDIENCE, AND THE DISTORTION OF THE RELATIONSHIP WITH GOD

The temptation of the devil and/or serpent in this situation was also moved by man's lack of trust in God the Creator. When the serpent tempted man, he let his trust in God die in his heart and then abused his freedom and disobeyed God.[66] Every sin after the original sin also has the component of the lack of trust in God's goodness.[67] They ended up believing in the serpent's deceit over God's instruction. Here, they lacked trust in God's wisdom.

Many people today have a lack of trust in the Church and turn away from God and the Church for many reasons they state today, such as accusing the church of misconduct, hypocrisy, that it is too strict, harboring intellectual doubts, etc. Sin here starts by not fully trusting God and not believing in His goodness or having doubts about His goodness and His moral order.

In the original sin, man denied God's moral order and preferred himself, which is what scorned God.[68] Man went against his creaturely status subject to the Moral Order of God and chose himself against his own good, denying his creatureliness and dependence upon the Creator.[69] Here, man

---

[66] Catholic Church. (2019). Catechism of the Catholic Church. Vatican City, Libreria Editrice Vaticana; Washington, D.C, para. 397, pg. 100

[67] Ibid

[68] Ibid, para. 398, pg. 100

[69] Ibid

was seduced by the devil, and according to the Catechism of the Catholic Church, "…he wanted to be like God, but without God, before God, and not in accordance with God. (Catechism, 2019, para. 398).[70] Here, man lost the state of grace or the original holiness and chose spiritual death and disobedience, meaning they fell from their once existing state of original holiness and justice.

This original justice and holiness were in perfect harmony with God, themselves, each other, and creation. Here, they lost the sense of grace, meaning they lost this perfect harmony, and the state of purity and innocence they once had was lost. Instead of their trust and love for God, it was now an era of fear and negative emotions toward God for their disobedient act. Here, instead of seeing God as a loving, generous Father, they began to see him as being jealous of His prerogatives, meaning they saw God as someone who was insecure about His own status and who wanted to keep them from becoming like Him. They believed by listening to the serpent that God was withholding something good from them, yet it was for their own protection and well-being; they believed His commands were out of jealousy and fear instead of protecting them from harm. This caused a fundamental change in their nature and relationship with God; their view of God became distorted, and they no longer were in harmony as they once were.[71]

---

[70] Ibid

[71] Ibid, para. 399, pg. 100

Carnal concupiscence is a morbid disposition in humans. It is a weakness that arouses unlawful desire, and because humans are generated and conceived in and through this carnal concupiscence, the flesh here becomes tainted, polluted, and corrupted; original sin is directly associated with the vice of concupiscence.[72] Before the fall of man, before original sin more clearly, man and woman could join together without the stain of sin, meaning without lust burning with concupiscence.[73] Because man is generated by the stain of lustful concupiscence, man's flesh becomes corrupted; it has the cause of sin, meaning in the altered human nature, there is vice.[74]

As the Holy Scripture explains, the spirit and the flesh war with each other, and in many cases, the soul is willing by the flesh is not able to meet the higher aspects of the soul, meaning the spirit may call one to do good, but the flesh drives one to vice in spite of the spirit calling to good. Thus, original sin is not in the soul; it becomes the corruption of the flesh because the cause of sin is in the flesh, because the flesh was generated in sin, and through this transmission, all flesh becomes that of sin. This is why the spirit wars against the flesh.[75] When God first designed humans, he did not taint them with vice, but they became wounded with vice because of the choice of our first parents, and because the flesh became corrupted and tainted,

---

[72] Peter Lombard, Sentences, Volume 2, Distinction XXX, Chapter 12, trans. Guilio Silano, (Toronto: Pontifical Institute of Mediaeval Studies, 2007), 154

[73] Peter Lombard, Sentences, Volume 2, Distinction XXX, Chapter 12, trans. Guilio Silano, (Toronto: Pontifical Institute of Mediaeval Studies, 2007), 154

[74] Peter Lombard, Sentences, Volume 2, Distinction XXX, Chapter 12, trans. Guilio Silano, (Toronto: Pontifical Institute of Mediaeval Studies, 2007), 155

[75] Ibid

the soul became corrupted.[76] Because of original sin, our parents joined together in lustful concupiscence, and it became a type of corruption of the flesh. Because this lust was infused in the act of procreation, it became a type of corruption of the flesh; this corruption is in the flesh even before the soul joins the body.

THE LEGACY OF ORIGINAL SIN: HUMANITY'S INHERITED WOUND AND THE PATH TO REDEMPTION

The reason why humanity is corrupted by original sin is because the whole human race is from the loins of Adam, the first human being. Adam's sin implicates the entire human race because all humans are now subject to spiritual and physical death and are all implicated in the justice of Christ.[77] In truth, original sin remains a mystery and cannot be fully understood, but what is known is that God intended original justice and holiness as a part of the original goodness of human nature that was intended as part of human nature as a whole. Because Adam and Eve committed personal sins, it affected human nature to a fallen state, and this fallen state became transmitted to the entire human posterity; thus, human nature became deprived of original justice and holiness.

When it comes to the sin being passed down to Adam's posterity, it means this sin passes down to the next posterity in a way that is contracted, not committed, meaning "a state and

---

[76] Ibid

[77] Catholic Church. (2019). Catechism of the Catholic Church. Vatican City, Libreria Editrice Vaticana; Washington, D.C, para. 404, pg. 102

not an act."[78] It is not a personal fault of people but a passed-down deprivation of original holiness and justice. It is a corruption of human nature, not a total corruption of human nature.[79] Our nature because of original sin is wounded in that it is subject to suffering, ignorance, death, and the inclination to sin, an evil inclination rightfully called concupiscence.[80]

Baptism erases original sin; it works to turn man back to God, but human nature remains somewhat weakened and inclined toward evil even after baptism. But man in the spiritual battle of life can be on the winning side through the grace of Christ and our cooperation with grace, the sacraments, and resisting evil temptation. Human beings, being creatures of God, cannot save themselves. In order to be saved, we must give up this false sense of autonomy and self-sufficiency, this false sense of living for ourselves alone, but become our true selves and accept that we are creatures of God in need of our Creator. We can be saved when we begin to engage in our proper relationships again, but this cannot truly occur until we once again unite with our creatureliness. Because our relations with the created world are broken, it takes an act of God Himself to save us and repair the network of relationships in the world.[81]

---

[78] Ibid, para. 405, pg. 102

[79] Ibid, para. 398, pg. 102

[80] Ibid

[81] Benedict, Pope. In the Beginning--: A Catholic Understanding of the Story of Creation and the Fall. Grand Rapids, Mich., W.B. Eerdmans Pub. Co, 1995, pg. 74

Chapter 3:

JESUS CHRIST'S SACRIFICE: THE ONLY REMEDY FOR ORIGINAL SIN

"If anyone asserts that the sin of Adam, which in its origin is one, and by propagation, not by imitation, transfused into all, which is in each one as something that is his own, is taken away either by the forces of human nature, or by a remedy other than the merit of the one mediator, our Lord Jesus Christ, who has reconciled us to God in his own blood, made unto us justice, sanctification and redemption; or if he denies that that merit of Jesus Christ is applied both to adults and to infants by the sacrament of baptism rightly administered in the form of the Church, let him be anathema; for there is no other name under heaven given to men, whereby we must be saved. Whence that declaration: <u>Behold the Lamb of God, behold him who taketh away the sins of the world, and that other: As many of you as have been baptized, have put on Christ.</u>" Council of Trent, Session 5, "Decree on Original Sin," Canon 3, in The Canons and Decrees of the Council of Trent, trans. H.J. Schroeder, (Rockford: Tan Books and Publishers, 1978), pg. 22)[82]

When Adam, the first human being, committed original sin, he injured his own self, but he also injured the entire human race, and because of original sin, because it altered human nature, all infants are tainted with this altered human nature of sin; *by one man sin entered into the world, and death by sin, and so death passed upon all*

---

[82] Council of Trent, Session 5, "Decree on Original Sin," Canon 3, in The Canons and Decrees of the Council of Trent, trans. H.J. Schroeder, (Rockford: Tan Books and Publishers, 1978), pg. 22)

men, in whom all sinned[83]. The fact is that human nature was ruined, and because of man's altered nature and weakness toward sin, the devil was able to take power over man and induce him to act contrary to his God-intended nature of original justice and holiness, but by Jesus Christ coming in the flesh to be sacrificed for our redemption, it works to deliver us from this fallen state, and we can only be delivered from this fallen state by the grace of the Redeemer; by the Lord Jesus Christ.[84]

The redemptive work of Jesus Christ primarily frees us from original sin and its consequences and restores us back into communion with God. We are in need of Jesus Christ to free us from original sin because through our own works, we cannot change the fallen nature we inherited, and because this fallen nature we inherited is in enmity with God, we cannot enter the Kingdom of Heaven with the fallen nature, and we need to be regenerated through Jesus Christ to reverse original sin so we can enter into the Kingdom of Heaven; *"Jesus answered: Amen, amen, I say to thee, unless a man be born again of water and the Holy Ghost, he cannot enter into the kingdom of God."*[85]

---

[83] Romans 5:12

[84] Augustine, and Aeterna Press. A Treatise on the Grace of Christ and on Original Sin. Aeterna Press, pg. 69

[85] John 3:5 (Douay-Rheims 1899 American Edition)

OVERCOMING ORIGINAL SIN: THE ROLE OF DIVINE GRACE AND THE SACRAMENTS

Because of original sin, human nature was altered, which gives man a strong inclination to sin, meaning an inclination to go against the spirit of chastity, temperance, charity, and genuine spiritual interests for the pursuance of carnal pleasures, lust, selfishness, and fleshly desires, which makes it impossible for man by his own power and freewill to truly fulfill all the Divine precepts. Man, by his own free will and power, does not have the ability to conquer all temptations and passions he will experience throughout life, and a person can only overcome the fallen nature, temptations, and passions by the grace bestowed upon man by Jesus Christ's sacrifice.[86]

This grace is given to us as a free gift that Christ procured for us by his death and sacrifice, and this grace cannot be obtained by our own works nor by our own strength; without grace, we cannot conquer the temptations that the stain of original sin has set upon all human souls. Although there are some remnants of original sin upon us, even after baptism, we still must resist temptations. Still, without Christ, the mediator, we could not resist these temptations upon our own power.[87]

Because of Adam's disobedience, Christ's obedience and His sacrifice are necessary for us to overcome the effects of original sin. As it is written in the Bible: *Behold the Lamb of God, behold Him Who taketh away the sin of the world*[88]. Sin is used in the

---

[86] Maria, Alfonso, and John Thomas Mullock. The History of Heresies, and Their Refutation, Or, the Triumph of the Church; Volume 1. Legare Street Press, pg. 99.

[87] Ibid

[88] John 1:29

singular context, not the plural, because it means to refer to original sin.[89] This sin, being original, deprived Adam's posterity of original justice and worked to corrupt our origins.[90] Because the nature of this altered nature is so strong within us, this strong sense of concupiscence, being that the world is full of temptations, we have strong internal conflicts because thereof. This is precisely why we need divine grace to overcome it. Sin is usually actions, but sin starts in the mind and spirit before the action takes place.

Because of original sin, we have a strong inclination to sin, and it is easy without divine grace to fall into sin because of the inclination to sin from the effects of original sin. Jesus's sacrifice was made to stop us from being slaves to sin so that the inclination to sin is almost eliminated. With reliance on divine grace, our cooperation with it, meaning to become part of the Church and partake in the sacraments (Eucharist, reconciliation, etc.), also by being vigilant and practicing self-control and adhering to Catholic moral teaching, we can once again reach a certain level of original justice and holiness in the way God intends in this life, that will prepare us for success in the next life.

Because Jesus set up His Church, we have the sacrament of reconciliation that gives us forgiveness after baptism and strengthens our resolve against sinful actions. We must use the tools God has given us in the way He intends in the physical

---

[89] Thomas Aquinas. Summa Theologiae: Prima Secundae Partis, Q. 82, Art. 2. Translated by the Fathers of the English Dominican Province, Aquinas Institute, Green Bay, WI, pg. 125

[90] Ibid, pg. 127

material world we live in. Because Christ gave the power to forgive sins to the Catholic Church in His Name, the way sin is forgiven in this physical, material world after baptism is through the sacrament of reconciliation. The bishops of today, as the successors of the Apostles, have been entrusted with the power to forgive sins. This authority stems directly from the commission Jesus gave to His Apostles. In John 20:21-23, Jesus said to them, *'As the Father has sent me, I am sending you.'* He then breathed on them and said, *'Receive the Holy Spirit. If you forgive anyone's sins, their sins are forgiven; if you do not forgive them, they are not forgiven.'*

As the Apostles' successors, the bishops carry on this sacred duty, exercising the same authority Christ bestowed upon the Apostles and the Church. Furthermore, this power to forgive sins is not merely symbolic; it is a real and effective grace that restores our relationship with God. In Matthew 16:19, Jesus also tells Peter, *'I will give you the keys of the kingdom of heaven; whatever you bind on earth will be bound in heaven, and whatever you loose on earth will be loosed in heaven.'* This binding and loosing authority, passed down through apostolic succession, ensures that the Church has the means to reconcile sinners with God. The sacrament of reconciliation is a gift of divine mercy, offering us the opportunity to repent and receive forgiveness. By participating in this sacrament, we are continually renewed in grace, strengthened to resist future temptations, and restored to full communion with the Body of Christ.

The relationship between Jesus Christ's Crucifixion and the sacrament of baptism is foundational to the Christian understanding of salvation. At the heart of this connection is the belief that through baptism, individuals are sacramentally united with Christ's death and resurrection. The Catechism of the Catholic Church emphasizes that baptism signifies and brings about a death to sin, allowing the baptized to enter into the life of the Most Holy Trinity. This sacramental act is deeply intertwined with the Paschal mystery of Christ, as believers are called to be buried with Him in baptism to rise with Him, thus participating in the new life He offers through His sacrifice on the Cross.[91]

The relationship between Jesus Christ's Crucifixion and the sacrament of baptism is foundational to the Christian understanding of salvation. At the heart of this connection is the belief that through baptism, individuals are sacramentally united with Christ's death and resurrection. The Catechism of the Catholic Church emphasizes that baptism signifies and brings about a death to sin, allowing the baptized to enter into the life of the Most Holy Trinity. This sacramental act is deeply intertwined with the Paschal mystery of Christ, as believers are called to be buried with Him in baptism to rise with Him, thus participating in the new life He offers through His sacrifice on the Cross.[92]

This union with Christ's death and resurrection through baptism is vividly expressed in Romans 6:3-4, where St. Paul

---

[91] Magisterium. (n.d.). [Title of the specific page]. Magisterium. https://www.magisterium.com/search/10875e99-f637-4186-a687-5ab1967d0442

[92] Magisterium. (n.d.). [Title of the specific page]. Magisterium. https://www.magisterium.com/search/10875e99-f637-4186-a687-5ab1967d0442

writes, '*Do you not know that all of us who have been baptized into Christ Jesus were baptized into His death? We were buried therefore with Him by baptism into death, in order that, just as Christ was raised from the dead by the glory of the Father, we too might walk in newness of life.*' Through this sacrament, the baptized are not only cleansed from original sin but are also reborn as children of God, becoming members of Christ's Body, the Church. This transformation is both a spiritual rebirth and a call to a new way of life, guided by the Holy Spirit. The graces received in baptism enable the faithful to live out their Christian vocation, striving for holiness and unity with God. It is through this sacramental initiation that believers are empowered to participate fully in the life of the Church and in the mission of spreading the Gospel to all nations.

Furthermore, the Crucifixion of Jesus is seen as the source of the grace that baptism imparts. The blood and water flowing from Christ's side during His Passion are understood as symbols of the sacraments of baptism and the Eucharist, which provide the means for believers to be reborn and enter the Kingdom of God. The Catechism states that everything that happened to Christ, including His death, allows for the possibility of being "born of water and the Spirit," highlighting how baptism is rooted in the redemptive act of the crucifixion. Thus, baptism is not merely a ritual but a profound participation in the life, death, and resurrection of Jesus, establishing a sacramental bond that links the baptized to the crucified and glorified Christ.

In essence, the act of baptism is a response to the love demonstrated in Christ's Crucifixion. It signifies a believer's commitment to live in accordance with the grace received through Christ's sacrifice, marking the beginning of a lifelong journey of faith. The sacrament invites individuals to embrace their identity as children of God, redeemed through the Cross, and to walk in the newness of life, reflecting the transformative power of Christ's death and resurrection in their daily lives.

THE STRUGGLE AGAINST THE FLESH AND THE REDEMPTION THROUGH CHRIST

Much of the New Testament speaks of man warring with the flesh against the Spirit. The sins of the flesh, primarily concupiscence, cause internal struggles for one to keep God's commandments. This altered human nature became a condition in which humans found themselves, and it is such a grievous altering of human nature that humans on their own could not and still cannot overcome it on their own, by their own works and wills. It can only be addressed from outside the human condition that something as awful must match the awfulness we are in, as a counterweight to the awfulness of sin, because sin is of a serious nature.

We know that Adam is the source of original sin, and we know the source of our redemption, i.e., Jesus Christ. We know that the serpent represented the devil and seduced Adam and Eve into sin and that Jesus Christ came to destroy the works of the devil in the physical material world that we live in. Holy Scripture tells us that by one man sin entered into the world, and by one's man righteousness, i.e., Jesus Christ, who being both fully human and fully God, brought acquittal for all men came into the world; original sin and the redemption found within Jesus Christ are universal, it applies to all men.[93]

Because of original sin, human nature itself weakened in its powers. Mankind came into an era of death, suffering, ignorance, and superstition and became a slave to sin, and being a slave to sin, the devil came into power over man, and Jesus Christ came into the world and willingly sacrificed himself to break the power of the devil over man and regenerate man into a new creation.[94] Our altered nature became stained with sin and corrupted, and it is in need of healing. Man cannot heal himself; we lost our original justice and holiness and needed a savior to give it back to us again. Here, Christ's death is the Paschal sacrifice that offers clear healing from the power and effects of original sin. Here, Jesus established the New Covenant, which works to restore man back into communion with God and reconcile him through Christ's blood and the establishment of the New Covenant.[95]

---

[93] Catholic Church. (2019). Catechism of the Catholic Church. Vatican City, Libreria Editrice Vaticana; Washington, D.C, para. 402, pg. 101

[94] Ibid, para. 415-421, pg. 105

[95] Ibid, para. 613, pg. 159

THE NECESSITY OF SACRIFICE FOR ATONEMENT: FROM OLD TESTAMENT RITUALS TO CHRIST'S ULTIMATE SACRIFICE

When the Old Testament is looked at, sacrificial offerings worked to bridge the gap between humans and God in terms of atonement and purification. In many cases, sacrifice is a predominant theme in the atonement and the forgiveness of sins in the Old Testament: Leviticus 17:11, which states, "For the life of the flesh is in the blood, and I have given it for you on the altar to make atonement for your souls, for it is the blood that makes atonement by the life." Whether it is taken to be literal or symbolic, what is evident is that the shedding of blood is serious because blood represents life, and because God associates atonement with the shedding of blood shows us how serious sin is in God's eyes, that it is not just forgiven easily, but requires a serious and significant act.

Before the coming of Christ, the Jewish nation had to practice Yom Kippur, where the High Priest would enter the Holy of Holies and sacrifice for the forgiveness of the sins of the whole Jewish nation. The sacrifice of Jesus Christ on the Cross represents the fulfillment and ultimate expression of the Hebrew Bible. Jesus represented the *Lamb of God who takes away the sin of the world* (John 1:29). His blood was shed for the ultimate atonement of mankind. It's rather gruesome when it comes to the shedding of blood, but necessary. *Without the shedding of blood there is no forgivene*ss (Hebrews 9:22). The beneficial thing about Jesus's sacrifice is that with his one in all sacrifice, the old sacrificial system has become transcended and no longer should be practiced. The old sacrificial system in the

Hebrew Bible was a precursor to the coming and sacrifice of Jesus Christ; Jesus's sacrifice was the final and perfect atonement for sin.

Many people today would say, why can't God simply remit original sin out of mercy alone without any accountability for the honor that was taken away from him? But in truth, this would equate to being the same as simply not punishing it all. Since original sin was so grievous that it literally altered human nature, it would not be appropriate to forgive it and bring it back to its God-intended state without compensation or satisfaction. If God were to simply forgive sin without punishment or satisfaction, it would be like not addressing the wrongdoing. Since God is a God of justice, if He simply allowed something inordinate to pass without satisfaction, this would mean that he would let things that are inordinate in His Kingdom pass. If He were to do this, He would not be a God of perfect justice; in essence, it is not fitting for God to remit sin without some type of punishment or satisfaction.[96]

We have the sacrament of reconciliation in the Church, but this is not for original sin. This is for sin after baptism (after entering into Christian life). Jesus's sacrifice is necessary for the forgiveness of original sin because, through his sacrifice, we are restored to communion with God and reconciled to Him by the blood of His Son, Jesus Christ. After baptism, if a person commits sin, it must be reconciled through the sacrament of reconciliation; this is necessary for the forgiveness of sins after

---

[96] Anselm (saint). Why God Became Man. Magi Publications, 1969, pg. 65

baptism. After baptism, a Christian must go to a Priest, confess their sins, perform contrition, and receive absolution. If one ponders, if sins go unpunished and those sins are remitted, a person who does not sin would be in the same position as one who does, and that would not work on the scales of justice before God.[97]

THE DISTINCTION AND ELEVATION OF HUMAN NATURE THROUGH DIVINE GRACE

God, being All Mighty, sent His Son into the world, meaning Jesus, being of the same substance as God, took on the lowliness and weakness of human flesh and nature to restore it.[98] The word became flesh so we can become partakers in divine nature, meaning we could now share in God's grace, which transforms and elevates our human nature without changing our essence so we can share in God's life and love.

The crucial distinction here is that human beings do not become gods in their own right because God is fundamentally different from human nature. Partaking in divine nature means that human beings are elevated and transformed by God's grace, but the Creator-creature distinction remains intact. This does not mean that human nature is equal to divine nature. Humans here remain distinct from God, even when they partake in the divine nature. This is important because people may take this teaching in the wrong way. Partaking in the divine nature does not imply some kind of pantheistic blending of God and creation. Rather, it highlights the profound and

---

[97] Anselm (saint). Why God Became Man. Magi Publications, 1969. pg. 86
[98] Ibid, pg. 65.

unique way in which God's grace interacts with human nature to bring about a new spiritual reality.

This transformation allows for a deeper communion with God while preserving the integrity of both divine and human natures. Thus, while we are drawn into a more intimate relationship with the divine, the sacred boundary between Creator and creature is maintained, ensuring that God's transcendence and our created distinctiveness are upheld. Ultimately, this relationship enriches human experience by providing a means to partake in divine holiness, fostering a dynamic and reciprocal relationship with God that uplifts human dignity without diminishing divine majesty. Through this grace, believers are empowered to live in harmony with divine will, reflecting the transformative power of God's love in their daily lives while remaining rooted in their created nature.

THE BONDAGE OF SIN AND THE REDEMPTION THROUGH CHRIST

Without God's redemption in Jesus Christ, man is held captive toward sin and by sin; *Whosoever committeth sin is the servant of sin* (John 8:34) and - *By whom a man is overcome, of the same also he is the slave* (2 Peter 2:19). Since the devil has induced man to sin, here man has become in bondage to the devil, and because of the consequences of Original Sin, mankind is stuck serving a debt of punishment from God's sense of justice, which is also a kind of bondage, meaning mankind is suck in suffering things he does not wish to suffer from.[99]

Because of original sin, humanity became stuck in a state of unrighteousness, meaning the lack of uprightness of will, which disallows us to reach a state of blessedness for which man was originally created.[100] According to St. Anselm, because of the miraculous way Jesus was born, being born of the Virgin Mary, he was born of the same substance as the Father but also the absence of carnal concupiscence, and here Jesus escapes original sin being in the flesh, here he escapes sin....[101] Because Adam was tainted with Original Sin being the first human, he could only transmit what was tainted.[102] This tainting is a defect affecting every soul; it is a congenital flaw.[103]

Because Jesus was born from a virgin and by the power of the Holy Spirit, he was born by other than ordinary human generation, even if He would not have been God in the flesh, he still would have been exempted from the tainting of original sin due to his miraculous birth.[104] But because of being free from the tainting of Original Sin and being God in the flesh, He became the source of our redemption. Because God willed

---

[99] "The object of anger is good or evil, because it seeks to inflict harm in response to perceived injustice." Summa Theologica. Translated by Fathers of the English Dominican Province, Second and Revised Edition, 1920, New Advent, https://www.newadvent.org/summa/4048.htm.

[100] Henri Rondet, Original Sin: The Patristic and Theological Background. Saint Pauls/Alba House, 1 Jan. 1972, pg. 144

[101] Henri Rondet, Original Sin: The Patristic and Theological Background. Saint Pauls/Alba House, 1 Jan. 1972, pg. 149

[102] Ibid

[103] Ibid

[104] Ibid

saintly mankind, but because man is corporeal and organic, man cannot separate his soul from the body. They both work together; here, human nature became tainted, meaning it became deprived of the original justice and holiness it was intended to have or once had.[105]

Man was made inherently or originally righteous. The condition was that man had to retain this righteousness and pass it on to his descendants. Here, every man should have been born in a state of original holiness and justice. Still, because Adam voluntarily chose to abandon this righteousness, all men must come into a world of unrighteousness.[106] This unrighteous state, rightfully called original sin, is a state of man that deserves damnation, and because it is remitted by baptism through the Redeemer, man can now receive redemption through the death and sacrifice of the Redeemer.[107] According to St. Thomas Aquinas, without the Redeemer, humanity is damned with a disordered sense of concupiscence as a consequence of original sin.[108]

---

[105] Ibid, pg. 155
[106] Ibid, pg. 157
[107] Ibid, pg. 155
[108] Ibid, pg. 163

THE ATONEMENT OF CHRIST: ANSELM'S SATISFACTION THEORY AND ITS IMPLICATIONS FOR ORIGINAL AND PERSONAL SIN

Jesus Christ, who is both fully divine and fully human, could adequately satisfy this debt. Jesus Christ, as God incarnate, possesses the infinite worth necessary to make amends for the infinite offense against God's honor caused by original sin. According to St. Anselm, his satisfaction theory hinges on the concept of justice and the restoration of order. God, being just, cannot simply overlook sin without compromising His justice. Therefore, satisfaction must be made to reconcile humanity with God. Jesus' voluntary sacrifice on the Cross is seen as the ultimate act of satisfaction. By willingly accepting death, Jesus offers a gift of infinite value to God, thereby restoring the disrupted order and repairing the relationship between humanity and the divine.

This act of atonement is not merely a transactional payment but a profound expression of love and justice, fulfilling the requirements of divine law. Through His sacrifice, Jesus not only pays the debt owed by humanity but also opens the way for humanity to be reconciled with God in a deeply personal and transformative way. This reconciliation is central to the Christian understanding of salvation, where Christ's atonement is seen as both a legal and relational restoration. The fruits of this sacrifice are accessible to all through the sacraments, particularly baptism, which incorporates individuals into the life of Christ and His Church. The satisfaction made by Christ is not just a past event but continues to have a real, ongoing effect in the lives of believers, who are called to live out this restored relationship in their daily lives. Thus, Jesus' atonement is the cornerstone of Christian faith, offering both the hope of eternal life and the means to live a life pleasing to God.

In relation to original sin, Anselm's theory underscores the necessity of Jesus's crucifixion for the eradication of the inherited guilt and corruption stemming from Adam's transgression. Original sin, according to traditional Christian doctrine, taints every human soul from birth, creating a chasm between God and humanity. Anselm asserts that this original guilt can be nullified only through Christ's sacrificial death. The crucifixion serves as a means to cleanse humanity of the inherited stain of sin, enabling believers to be reconciled with God and restoring the potential for eternal life. Thus, Anselm's satisfaction theory provides a compelling theological framework for understanding the significance of Jesus's crucifixion in the context of original sin. It emphasizes the necessity of divine justice being met through the perfect sacrifice of Christ, who bridges the gap between God and humanity. This act of atonement not only addresses the individual sins of believers but also the collective burden of original sin, offering a path to redemption and eternal communion with God.[109]

Anselm of Canterbury's views on personal sin committed after baptism are intricately linked to his understanding of original sin and the necessity of Christ's atonement. While baptism, in Anselm's view, cleanses an individual from original

---

[109] Anselm (saint). Why God Became Man. Magi Publications, 1969

sin and initiates them into a state of grace, it does not render them immune to subsequent personal sin. Anselm acknowledges that baptized Christians remain susceptible to sin due to their human nature and the lingering effects of concupiscence, the inclination to sin that persists even after the stain of original sin is removed. Personal sins committed after baptism disrupt the relationship with God that baptism has restored. However, Anselm emphasizes that Christ's atonement on the Cross provides ongoing grace and the means for reconciliation. Through sincere repentance and the sacrament of confession, baptized individuals can receive forgiveness for their post-baptismal sins, restoring their communion with God. This continual reliance on Christ's sacrificial satisfaction highlights the enduring nature of God's grace and the importance of the sacraments in the spiritual life of a Christian. Anselm's perspective underscores the perpetual need for divine mercy and Christ's atonement's transformative power in addressing original and personal sin.

Chapter 4:

THEOLOGICAL BASIS FOR BAPTIZING INFANTS TO REMOVE ORIGINAL SIN

If anyone denies that infants, newly born from their mothers' wombs, are to be baptized, even though they be born of baptized parents, or says that they are indeed baptized for the remission of sins, but that they derive nothing of original sin from Adam which must be expiated by the layer of regeneration for the attainment of eternal life, whence it follows that in them the form of baptism for the remission of sins is to be understood not as true but as false, let him be anathema, for what the Apostle has said, by one man sin entered into the world, and by sin death, and so death passed upon all men, in whom all have sinned, is not to be understood otherwise than as the Catholic Church has everywhere and always understood it. For in virtue of this rule of faith handed down from the apostles, even infants who could not as yet commit any sin of themselves, are for the reason truly baptized for the remission of sins, in order that in them what they contracted by generation may be washed away by regeneration. For, unless a man be born again of water and the Holy Ghost, he cannot enter into the kingdom of heaven. (Council of Trent, Session 5, "Decree on Original Sin," Canon 4, in The Canons and Decrees of the Council of Trent, trans. H.J. Schroeder, (Rockford: Tan Books and Publishers, 1978), pg. 22).[110]

---

[110] Council of Trent, Session 5, "Decree on Original Sin," Canon 4, in The Canons and Decrees of the Council of Trent, trans. H.J. Schroeder, (Rockford: Tan Books and Publishers, 1978), pg. 22)

The question many people have when pondering original sin is that when both parents become baptized, and a baby is born because the parents are both baptized, it is commonly deduced that the child would not need baptism because both parents were baptized. However, the Church ruled in the earliest centuries when this controversy first sprang up, stating that babies still need baptism even if the parents were both baptized. Analogies the early theologians used that of circumcision: even though a person becomes cleansed through circumcision, a son still inherits the foreskin that is later circumcised. Another analogy is that the chaff is removed from a grain through human labor yet reappears in a new grain produced from winnowed wheat. Parents here don't beget children from their renewed spiritual nature; they are according to the original carnal nature, and using the analogies, they are still born in original sin that persists in the flesh.[111]

In truth, all people are born from the loins of Adam, the first human being, and because of this, all people are born with the corrupted flesh from the sin of Adam. Because being born of corrupted flesh, the devil has unduly power over humanity, and even infants are not born stainless.[112] When it comes to original sin, every soul that is born is born pertaining to Adam until it belongs to Christ. If it belongs to Adam, it is sinful and unclean.[113] It does not mean that man cannot be good even though sullied by original sin; he simply has the original defect

---

[111] Peter Lombard, Sentences, Volume 2, Distinction XXX, Chapter 12, trans. Guilio Silano, (Toronto: Pontifical Institute of Mediaeval Studies, 2007), 156

[112] Henri Rondet, Original Sin: *The Patristic and Theological Background*. Saint Pauls/Alba House, 1 Jan. 1972, pg. 59

[113] Ibid

within him: vitiumorigin is, which is Latin for defect of origin.[114]

Here, humans stained by original sin tend to have a dual nature because they have a tendency toward sin. They often do both good and bad. Once baptism comes into the picture, it erases the dual nature and makes them whole or one; it works to reconcile the dual nature sullied by original sin.[115] This does not mean human beings can do whatever they want after baptism. People must cooperate with the grace one receives after baptism in so far as to, at the very least, avoid mortal sin. Baptism removes the stain of original sin, but it does not fully eliminate the inclination to sin, known as concupiscence, which remains a challenge throughout a person's life. This inclination is a reminder of the ongoing spiritual battle each baptized person must engage in to live a life of virtue.

The sacrament of baptism grants the grace necessary to resist sin, but it also calls for a continual commitment to follow Christ and to grow in holiness. Thus, while baptism makes one spiritually whole, the journey toward complete sanctification requires constant effort, prayer, and reliance on God's grace. The sacraments, especially the Eucharist and Reconciliation, provide ongoing support for the faithful, helping them to remain in communion with God and to persevere in the path of righteousness.

---

[114] Ibid
[115] Ibid

According to the Council of Carthage, when it comes to infants, it does not mean that the infant has committed personal sin. It means they are still responsible for Adam's transgression in the way that they have the effects of original sin in them, and they undergo the penalty of Adam's transgression. This is why they are baptized as infants, to erase the effects of original sin in them; In John 3:5 it says: *For unless a man be born again of water and the Holy Ghost, he cannot enter into the kingdom of heaven.* The grace of God is not because of our merits; it is freely given, meaning we cannot overcome original sin by our own actions. It must be overcome by baptism, even though the infant has not committed personal sin yet. Through the sacrament of baptism, the infant is cleansed of original sin and becomes a new creation in Christ.

This foundational doctrine underscores the importance of grace and the necessity of sacraments in the life of the Church. Baptism, therefore, is not merely a ritual but a vital means of grace, ensuring that the soul is restored to a state of sanctifying grace, free from the inherited stain of original sin. Through baptism, the infant is not only cleansed but also initiated into theChristian community, becoming a member of the Body of Christ. This sacrament marks the beginning of the child's spiritual journey, providing the foundation for a life of faith and discipleship. The Church, following the teachings of the early councils like the Council of Carthage, emphasizes that baptism is necessary for salvation, as it imparts the Holy Spirit and unites the baptized with Christ's death and resurrection. As the child grows, the graces received in baptism continue to work within them, enabling them to resist sin and grow in virtue.

This transformative process highlights the profound impact of baptism, which is not just a cleansing from sin but a rebirth into a new life in Christ.

CHAPTER 5:

CONCUPISCENCE AFTER BAPTISM: STRUGGLE AND REWARD

If anyone denies by the grace of our Lord Jesus Christ which is conferred in baptism, the guilt of original sin is remitted, or says that the whole of that which belongs to the essence of sin is not taken away, but says that it is only canceled or not imputed, Let him be anathema. For in these who are born again God hates nothing, because there is no condemnation to those who are truly buried together with Christ by baptism, unto death, who walk not according to the flesh, but, putting off the old man and putting on the new one who is created according to God, are made innocent, immaculate, pure, guiltless and beloved of God, heirs indeed of God, joint heirs with Christ, so that there is nothing whatever to hinder their entrance into heaven. But this holy council perceives and confesses that in the one baptized there remains concupiscence or an inclination to sin, which, since it is left for us to wrestle with, cannot injure those who do not acquiesce but resist manfully by the grace of Jesus Christ; indeed, he who shall have striven lawfully shall be crowned. This concupiscence, which the Apostle sometimes calls sin, the holy council declares the Catholic Church has never understood to be called sin in the sense that it is truly and properly sin in those born again, but in the sense that it is of sin and inclines to sin. But if anyone is on the contrary opinion, let him be anathema.

This holy council declares, however, that it is not its intention to include this decree, which deals with original sin, the blessed and immaculate Virgin Mary, the mother of God, but that the constitutions of Pope Sixtus IV, of happy memory, are to be observed under the penalties contained in these constitutions, which it renews. (Council of Trent, Session 5, "Decree on Original Sin," Canon 5, in The Canons and Decrees of the Council of Trent, trans. H.J. Schroeder, (Rockford: Tan Books and Publishers, 1978), pg. 23).[116]

THE ONGOING NATURE OF CHRIST'S REDEMPTION: UNDERSTANDING THE ROLE OF SACRAMENTS, GRACE, AND RECONCILIATION IN CATHOLIC DOCTRINE

What is commonly misunderstood, especially by Protestants, is that Christ's redemptive work did not end with His Crucifixion. It remains ongoing long after up until this very day till the end of time. Redemption lies in cooperating with grace, meaning establishing a mystical union with Christ through His sacraments...Baptism, Eucharist, Reconciliation, etc. Jesus Christ's sacrifice, believing that being granted the Holy Spirit restores human nature to its original state before the fall, in the way of restoring the relationship between God and humanity, thus granting the possibility of eternal life; the reason for the possibility is that it is up to human beings to cooperate with sanctifying grace by living righteously, resisting vice and sin, and fulfilling the sacraments.

Many Protestants who are deceived believe that one cannot lose sanctifying grace after baptism, and often, many believe that they can commit as many sins as they please after baptism and believe they will be forgiven because Christ's Crucifixion covers all our sins. In truth, Christ's sacrifice cancels out Original Sin, restores our fallen nature to our original nature, frees us from

---

[116] Council of Trent, Session 5, "Decree on Original Sin," Canon 5, in The Canons and Decrees of the Council of Trent, trans. H.J. Schroeder, (Rockford: Tan Books and Publishers, 1978), pg. 23)

being a slave to sin, and nearly stops all the inclination toward evil as we once had before, but it does not cancel out sin that we do personally after baptism.

In Catholic teaching, the understanding of sin, particularly mortal sin, after baptism is crucial to the faith. Catholic doctrine distinguishes between venial sins, which are lesser sins that weaken but do not sever a person's relationship with God, and mortal sins, which are grave offenses that lead to a complete separation from God's grace. For a sin to be considered mortal, it must involve serious matter, be committed with full knowledge of its gravity, and be done with deliberate consent. Mortal sin results in the loss of sanctifying grace, the divine life that enables a person to share in the life and love of God. If a person dies in a state of unrepented mortal sin, Catholic doctrine teaches that they will be condemned to hell, understood as eternal separation from God. *Know you not that the unjust shall not possess the kingdom of God? According to* 1 Corinthians 6:9-10 (DRA): *Do not err: neither fornicators, nor idolaters, nor adulterers, Nor the effeminate, nor liers with mankind, nor thieves, nor covetous, nor drunkards, nor railers, nor extortioners shall possess the kingdom of God.*

To restore the state of grace after committing a mortal sin, a Catholic must participate in the sacrament of confession, which involves contrition (sincere sorrow for sin with the intention of not sinning again), confession (telling one's sins to a priest), absolution (the priest absolving the person of their sins), and penance (performing acts assigned by the priest as amends for the sins committed). This sacrament provides the very means to restore the state of grace within the soul and communion with the Church and the community once again.[117] For those who die in a state of grace but still need purification from venial sins or the temporal effects of sin, the doctrine of Purgatory provides a period of purification before entering Heaven.

This comprehensive framework emphasizes the seriousness of sin, the importance of reconciliation, and the continuous need for repentance and God's mercy. The sacrament of confession, therefore, is not just a momentary act but an ongoing process of spiritual renewal and growth in holiness. It reinforces the believer's relationship with God and the Church, reminding them of the need for humility and the grace of forgiveness. Regular participation in this sacrament helps Catholics remain vigilant against sin and encourages a life of virtue and charity. The practice of penance, which often includes prayer, fasting, and almsgiving, further deepens the individual's commitment to conversion and spiritual healing. Ultimately, this sacramental life is designed to prepare the soul for eternal union with God, fostering a deeper understanding of divine mercy and the path to salvation.

---

[117] To the participants in the course on the internal Forum organized by the Apostolic Penitentiary (March 31, 2001)

THE LIMITS OF SOLA FIDE: THE NECESSITY OF RECONCILIATION AND THE SACRAMENTAL ECONOMY IN ADDRESSING POST-BAPTISMAL SIN

In contrast, many Protestant denominations hold to the belief in salvation by faith alone (sola fide). They teach that once a person has faith in Jesus Christ, they are justified and saved. This justification is a one-time event that covers all sins—past, present, and future. Protestant theology often rejects the distinction between mortal and venial sins and the necessity of the sacrament of confession, instead advocating for direct repentance to God. Protestants believe that faith and repentance are ongoing aspects of the Christian life but view salvation as secure for those who have genuine faith.

Many people in the Protestant circles believe that once a person is saved, they are eternally secure in salvation regardless of the sin they commit, even after baptism. Protestants often focus on a personal relationship with Christ through grace, while traditional Catholics engage in a sacramental economy of the Church as a means of grace. The problem with their heresy is that it hurts them greatly and severely affects their chances for true redemption and success in the afterlife.

Even though the sacrifice of Jesus Christ effectively cancels out original sin through the sacrament of baptism, it does not completely cancel out all the effects of original sin in human nature. Some of the effects of original sin remain after baptism, meaning some of the inclination to sin (concupiscence) remains, and if followed, it can lead a person to the loss of divine grace and sever a person with communion with the Church. Because some of the effects are still present even after baptism, this requires spiritual and moral vigilance, and the use of the sacraments is the perfect remedy for the effects of original sin after baptism.

According to Bellarmine, "...the Seven Sacraments are necessary because they are the instruments whereby we might recoup and preserve the virtue which we already said was necessary to salvation" (pg. 2).[118] For example, practicing the sacraments of reconciliation and the Eucharist work to continuously nourish the faithful which strengthens them against the temptations that arise from the effects of original sin, i.e., concupiscence. Baptism restores our relationship with God, but the faithful must continually seek grace through the sacraments to navigate life and succeed amid the negative effects of original sin.

By Protestants denying that one can lose sanctifying grace after baptism and denying the sacraments, they are only harming themselves because they are fighting a losing battle. They don't have the sacraments to give them the power to fight the temptations from the effects of original sin after baptism. According to Matthew 7:21-23, Jesus states that *not everyone who says to me, 'Lord, Lord,' will enter the kingdom of heaven, but only the one who does the will of my Father in heaven.* By denying the sacraments in a world full of temptations, still with some of the effects of original sin, without the Catholic Church and

---

[118] Bellarmine, Robert, et al. Doctrina Christiana: The Timeless Catechism of St. Robert Bellarmine. Lulu.com, 28 Sept. 2016, pg. 2

sacraments, and the arrogance many protestants have against the Catholic Church and sacraments, in reality, they are only hurting their own chances of salvation.

Considering original sin and the effect thereof, baptism washes away original sin. It infuses the soul with Sanctifying Grace, which works to regenerate a person into a new creation and once again restores that person to a proper relationship with God. Once a person is baptized, given the Holy Spirit, and has knowledge of good and evil according to God's understanding and moral system, a person sinning after baptism can be much more serious than a person committing sin without baptism, Holy Spirit, and Sanctifying Grace.

This is one of the reasons why the Protestant heresy is so serious, because some of the effects of original sin are still present in us, and with the world full of temptations, such as pornography, engaging in sin after baptism is even more serious for the person who accepted Christ over the person who has not. A person who has not been baptized remains fully affected by original sin, which means they have a strong tendency to sin because their nature is still corrupted.

In contrast, a baptized person has received sanctifying grace and the Holy Spirit, which helps them resist sin and guides their understanding of good and evil according to God's will. The inclination to sin is significantly less for the baptized person due to these divine aids, if they commit a serious sin with full knowledge and deliberate consent, their guilt is greater than that of someone who is not baptized. This is because they are held to a higher standard of responsibility due to the grace and guidance they have received. Thus, sinning after baptism is considered more serious because of the greater moral and spiritual insights granted by the Holy Spirit and sanctifying grace.

A non-baptized person is fully affected by original sin, meaning they are still subject to strong sinful inclinations. In contrast, a baptized person has their original sin removed, receives sanctifying grace, and is given the Holy Spirit along with His seven gifts (wisdom, understanding, counsel, fortitude, knowledge, piety, and fear of the Lord). Because the baptized person's inclination to sin is much less due to these blessings, someone who believes that all sins are automatically forgiven after baptism and continues to sin without seeking reconciliation through the sacrament is in a more serious state of condemnation than someone who is not baptized. This is why the Protestant heresy of Sola Fide, which claims that faith alone is sufficient for salvation and ignores the need for reconciliation, is considered a particularly dangerous error.

After baptism, there is still a struggle with concupiscence, and our actions after baptism can have serious consequences depending on our knowledge and intent. Sinning after baptism actually puts Christians into greater responsibility for their sins, because baptism empowers people to live according to God's will, and failing to do so can lead to more severe punishment. It is obvious that a non-Christian who sins out of ignorance may not face the same level of accountability as a baptized individual who knowingly rejects God's commandments.

Here, Protestants are greatly deceived because they are not forgiven for their sins after baptism, and this sectarian, dismissive, contemptuous, treasonous attitude they have toward the Catholic Church and the sacraments only increases their accountability by refusing to adhere to the Church Christ set up upon the rock of St. Peter by Christ Himself. By Protestants denying and turning away from the Catholic Church and the sacraments, they, in truth, are only turning away from "the instruments whereby we might recoup and preserve the virtue which we already said was necessary to salvation."

Many Protestants would say that when a Christian commits mortal sin after baptism, all they must do is make an informal request for forgiveness, and that is sufficient. In truth, God is a Perfect Being of Perfect Justice and Mercy. In regard to sin, it must align with His nature of upholding divine law and order. When a person commits a mortal sin, he or she is seriously breaching and violating His divine order. Because of the seriousness of sin after baptism, a mere informal request for forgiveness cannot be achieved this way.

For forgiveness after baptism, since the sin or matter is even more grave because it was done after baptism, it requires a more structured formal process that reflects the seriousness of the offense and the gravity of reparation. Mortal Sin destroys the sanctifying grace within the soul, and a mere informal request of forgiveness more than likely will not restore sanctifying grace within the soul after the mortal sin. The formal way to seek forgiveness after baptism for sin, especially mortal sin, is through the sacrament of reconciliation.

Confession in the Catholic Church is not a human invention; it was established by Christ Himself through the Church and priesthood, proved by John 20:22-23 (DRA): *And when he had said this, he breathed on them; and he said to them: Receive ye the Holy Ghost. Whose sins you shall forgive, they are forgiven them; and whose sins you shall retain, they are retained.* The priest here forgiving sins is not acting in his own accord; he is acting in persona Christi (in the person of Christ), and it is Christ who forgives sins through this sacramental action. The priest is being used as a divine instrument.

After baptism, a person becomes endowed with sanctifying grace. Here, the doer of mortal sin is more grievous since they have consciously rejected grace and the responsibilities given through baptism and the Holy Spirit. Because baptism gives Christians the means to resist sin, failing to do so only increases the degree of culpability. By denying and dismissing the sacraments, Protestants only increase their own accountability and severely harm their own spiritual well-being. *For if we sin wilfully after that we have received the knowledge of the truth, there remaineth no more sacrifice for sins,* (Hebrews 10:26-27 DRA).

After baptism, individuals receive sanctifying grace and the Holy Spirit, which effectively cancels the effects of original sin and restores them to a state of grace as children of God. This profound transformation places a greater responsibility on the baptized to live according to this new life in Christ. When a baptized person commits a mortal sin, it is more serious. They are held to a higher standard than someone who has not received these graces, as they have willingly chosen to turn away from the divine life they have been given.

The Protestant notion of sola fide ("faith alone"), which posits that faith alone suffices for salvation, falls short in addressing the gravity of post-baptismal sin. It does not account for the necessity of a formal process of reconciliation, which the Catholic Church teaches is essential for restoring one's relationship with God after serious sin. The sacrament of reconciliation, instituted by Christ, provides the formal and structured means through which the sinner can acknowledge their wrongdoing, express true contrition, and receive absolution, thereby re-entering into the fullness of sanctifying grace and to reaffirm to live according to God's will. This sacramental economy underscores the importance of community and the Church's role in the believer's journey of faith, ensuring that the grace of God is actively at work in the life of the faithful. This sacrament properly addresses the gravity of post-baptismal sin, which alights with divine justice and mercy established by Christ.

Chapter 6:
OVERCOMING THE CARNAL NATURE

The calamity of original sin introduced humankind to concupiscence—a carnal inclination that has endured in our nature since the disobedience of Adam and Eve. Though baptism restores us to sanctifying grace, reversing our fallen state and regenerating us as new creations, it does not wholly eradicate this inclination, leaving behind traces as both a testament to our fall and a test for our sanctification. Through the redemptive sacrifice of Christ, the wisdom of Sacred Scripture, and the guidance of classical Christian doctrine, we discern that the conquest of concupiscence is a lifelong endeavor, demanding our steadfast cooperation with divine grace. This includes vigilance, frequenting the sacraments, growth in faith and sanctity, and a disciplined spirit of self-mastery.

THE ORIGIN AND CONSEQUENCES OF CARNAL NATURE

Our carnal nature—the pronounced inclination toward sin, especially sins of the flesh—finds its origin in the fall of our first parents, Adam and Eve. Their choice to turn from God wrought profound consequences, corrupting human nature and exposing us to disorder, disease, and death. St. Augustine speaks of this as the "wound of original sin." Through baptism, this wound is healed as our souls are reordered toward God;

yet, it does not erase every mark of the fall, leaving within us a proclivity to sin. This tendency serves as both a reminder of our fallen state and a call to grow in virtue. Thus, we are bound to guard vigilantly against concupiscence as we advance on our path to holiness.

THE ROLE OF DIVINE GRACE IN OVERCOMING CONCUPISCENCE

Recognizing the depths of our frailty reveals our utter dependence on divine assistance. St. Paul captures this inner struggle when he says, "I do not understand what I do. For what I want to do, I do not do, but what I hate, I do" (Romans 7:15). This passage unveils the conflict within the human soul, a struggle that cannot be conquered by human strength alone. Through the sacrificial act of Christ, grace entered history, and by the power of His sacrifice, we are renewed through baptism.

Yet, even after baptism, the conquest over concupiscence is not of our own merit but remains reliant upon God's continued grace. While we are called to vigilance—frequenting the sacraments, nurturing virtue, and avoiding sin—these efforts require our cooperation with grace through faith and works. Through this union of divine aid and our response, we gradually overcome the inclinations of the flesh that seek to draw us from God, advancing steadily toward true holiness.

THE SACRED PURPOSE OF SEXUALITY

The Church teaches that sexuality is a sacred gift, intended as an act of love reflecting God's creative power. In accordance with Humanae Vitae, sexuality finds its rightful place within the sacramental bond of marriage, where it remains open to the gift of new life. When sexual acts occur outside this sacred context or are altered through the use of contraception—even within marriage—the true purpose of sexuality is obscured. As Humanae Vitae affirms, such distortions hinder the fullness of this divine design:

"The Church, nevertheless, in urging men to the observance of the precepts of the natural law, which it interprets by its constant doctrine, teaches that each and every marital act must of necessity retain its intrinsic relationship to the procreation of human life" (Humanae Vitae, 11).[119]

Further, Pope Pius XI in Casti Connubii teaches that contraception defies the natural purpose of the marital act:

"Since, therefore, the conjugal act is destined primarily by nature for the begetting of children, those who in exercising it deliberately frustrate its natural power and purpose sin against nature and commit a deed which is shameful and intrinsically vicious.

Small wonder, therefore, if Holy Writ bears witness that the Divine Majesty regards with greatest detestation this horrible crime and at times has punished with death. As St. Augustine

---

[119] Pope Paul VI. (1968, July 25). Humanae Vitae. www.vatican.va.

notes, "Intercourse even with one's legitimate wife is unlawful and wicked where the conception of the offspring are prevented. Onan, the son of Judah, did this and the Lord killed him for it."

Since, therefore, openly departing from the uninterrupted Christian tradition some recently have judged it possible solemnly to declare another doctrine regarding this question, the Catholic Church, to whom God has entrusted the defense of the integrity and purty of morals, standing erect in the midst of the moral ruin which surrounds her, in order that she may preserve the chastity of the nuptial union from being defiled by this foul stain, raises her voice in token of her divine ambassadorship and through Our mouth proclaims anew: any use whatsoever of matrimony exercised in such a way that the act is deliberately frustrated in its natural power to generate life is an offense against the law of God and of nature, and those who indulge in such are branded with the guilt of grave sin. (CC 54-6)."[120]

The Catholic Church teaches that contraception diminishes the sacred nature of marital union, reducing it to a pursuit of pleasure that severs it from its God-given procreative purpose. Contraception fosters a culture where sexuality is practiced primarily for self-gratification, neglecting the profound significance of love and life-creation intended by God. In contrast, the Church supports Natural Family Planning (NFP) methods—such as the Sympto-Thermal Method, the Billings

---

[120] Coffin, P. (2018). The contraception deception: Catholic teaching on birth control. Emmaus Road Publishing.

Ovulation Method, and the Calendar Rhythm Method—which honor the natural rhythms of fertility and respect God's design, enabling couples to space births without compromising the procreative essence of the marital act. This approach upholds human dignity and preserves the fullness of marital love.

According to sound Catholic teaching on sexual morality, sexual acts are morally licit only within the sacred bond of sacramental marriage between a man and a woman, and these acts must remain open to the possibility of life, free from artificial contraception. Any sexual act outside of sacramental marriage is considered gravely immoral, and within marriage, the use of contraception likewise renders the act morally grave by obstructing its natural openness to life. This teaching upholds the dual purpose of marital sexuality—unity and procreation—and preserves its sanctity by aligning it with God's divine intention.

The Catholic Church teaches that each marital act should remain open to the possibility of life. This means that any deliberate action to prevent the potential for procreation, often referred to as "spilling the seed," contradicts the purpose of marital intimacy as God intended. Sexual union within marriage has a dual purpose: to express love and unity between the spouses and to participate in God's creative power through openness to life. When a marital act is intentionally closed off from the potential for life—whether through contraceptive methods or actions that deliberately waste the procreative element—it reduces this union to mere personal satisfaction and separates it from its sacred role in life-giving love.

This teaching calls spouses to see their union as an expression of both love and potential parenthood, mirroring God's love by remaining open to His creative will. In respecting this purpose, couples honor the natural design and dignity of human sexuality, which goes beyond individual pleasure to participate in God's plan for family and human flourishing.

REJECTING IMPURITY: PORNOGRAPHY, MASTURBATION, AND LUSTFUL BEHAVIOR

In a world that normalizes and even glorifies impurity, Catholics are called to pursue radical purity. Pornography, masturbation, and other lustful behaviors degrade the sanctity of sexuality, fueling concupiscence and corrupting the mind. To overcome this, we must reject these distortions and actively avoid images, ideas, or environments that incite lust. St. Paul exhorts us to "think on things that are true, noble, and pure" (Philippians 4:8), and by focusing our minds on these virtues, we can cultivate purity in place of impurity.

THE SACRAMENT OF RECONCILIATION: ESSENTIAL FOR OVERCOMING CONCUPISCENCE

Concupiscence is a persistent challenge, and our weaknesses can often lead to failure. However, the Sacrament of Penance offers us a way back to God. Frequent confession strengthens our resolve and draws more grace, which helps us resist future temptations. For grave sins, especially those against chastity like fornication, adultery, pornography or masturbation, the Church requires Catholics to seek Reconciliation before receiving the Eucharist. The Catechism teaches:

"Anyone conscious of a grave sin must receive the Sacrament of Reconciliation before coming to communion" (CCC 1457).

Receiving the Eucharist in a state of mortal sin is a sacrilege, as St. Paul warns:

"Whoever, therefore, eats the bread or drinks the cup of the Lord in an unworthy manner will be guilty of profaning the body and blood of the Lord. Let a man examine himself, and so eat of the bread and drink of the cup. For anyone who eats and drinks without discerning the body eats and drinks judgment upon himself" (1 Corinthians 11:27-29).

Confession not only restores our relationship with God but also strengthens our commitment to purity, healing the wounds caused by sin and enabling us to approach the Eucharist with a clean heart.

The struggle to overcome concupiscence can feel daunting, especially when the roots of these tendencies have been nourished over years or even decades. Habits formed through repeated sin can seem deeply entrenched, making each slip feel like a failure and often tempting us to give up in shame. Yet, God's mercy is boundless, and His invitation to forgiveness remains open to us without limit. We must resist the urge to retreat into shame; rather, we are called to humbly and courageously return to confession as often as needed, trusting in God's grace to strengthen us with each absolution.

This journey may be long, requiring persistent effort and many returns to the sacrament. But do not allow setbacks to discourage you. True victory over sin lies in perseverance and the continued turning of the heart toward God, regardless of how many times we falter. Confession is not a sign of defeat but a testament to our commitment to pursue holiness. In every act of repentance, we chip away at the power of concupiscence, growing stronger in virtue and closer to the purity to which we are called. Never abandon this fight; trust that God's grace will uphold you, for in His eyes, every step back to Him is a victory.

GUARDING THE MIND AND RESISTING TEMPTATION

It is important to understand that a fleeting sexual thought is not a sin; sin enters when we choose to dwell on it with lustful intent. The Church Fathers taught that the mind must be guarded like a garden, cultivated with virtue and protected from harmful thoughts. When such thoughts arise, we should consciously redirect our attention to something virtuous, such as prayer or meditating on God's love.

Frequent confession, even for what may seem like minor sins, fortifies us against more severe temptations, helping us grow stronger in virtue. If we choose to dwell on a lustful thought, it becomes a sin, and we should seek reconciliation to purify our hearts and prevent this from leading to greater acts of lust. It is natural to notice beauty, such as seeing a beautiful woman, but it is wrong to linger and stare, as this invites temptation and weakens our resolve toward chastity.

Dwelling on sexual thoughts—entertaining or lingering upon them—is distinct from experiencing fleeting or unbidden thoughts. While the presence of these thoughts is not inherently sinful, choosing to dwell on them leads us into sin, as it opens the heart to concupiscence and weakens our resolve against more serious temptations. By nurturing these thoughts, we invite impurity to take root, making it harder to resist the allure of greater sins.

Regular confession for dwelling on these thoughts helps guard the soul by cultivating vigilance and humility. This act of repentance not only cleanses us but strengthens our ability to reject these distractions, reinforcing our commitment to purity. Each confession renews our defenses, making us more alert to these temptations and equipping us with the grace to turn our minds back to God. Through this sacrament, we fortify our hearts against both lesser and greater sins, nurturing purity in thought and deed.

RESTORING BAPTISMAL PURITY: OVERCOMING THE CARNAL NATURE THROUGH GRACE AND VIRTUE

In overcoming the carnal nature, one must recognize that the inordinate sex drive often perceived as "natural" is in reality a byproduct of our own actions and inclinations post-baptism. By dwelling upon and engaging in concupiscence—those acts and thoughts that gratify desires outside the bounds of God's will—we foster and intensify this misdirected impulse. However, when we cease to practice concupiscence and earnestly seek the Sacrament of Reconciliation, we invite grace back into our lives, and this grace—through cooperation in the sacraments—helps to restore our baptismal holiness.

By pursuing a life of virtue, aligning with righteousness, and consciously avoiding sin, the false sense of an uncontrollable sex drive diminishes. What remains is a pure, natural inclination toward procreation, a desire aligned with divine purpose, but without the burden of lust. In this state, the holiness granted at baptism can be fully experienced, as the seed of concupiscence, no longer nourished, gradually withers away, allowing true spiritual freedom to flourish.

THE DEVIL'S TOOLS IN TEMPTING US TO SEXUAL SIN: THE DANGERS OF SECLUSION AND SENSORY MANIPULATION

According to classical Catholic teaching, the devil employs several tools to lead us into sexual sin, exploiting our weaknesses and tendencies to draw us away from virtue. One primary tactic is isolation or seclusion, creating an environment where we are left alone with our thoughts, far from the guiding influence of community, accountability, and grace-filled relationships. In seclusion, we become vulnerable, as the devil plants and nurtures thoughts and desires that are easier to combat in the light of fellowship and prayer. Isolation makes us more susceptible to self-centered impulses, stripping away the support structures that help to guard purity.

Additionally, he uses deception by presenting sinful temptations as harmless or justified, distorting our view of chastity and virtue. The devil also manipulates our senses, particularly through the imagery and media we consume, to subtly desensitize us to sin and stoke desires that are contrary to God's will. These tools collectively serve his aim: to undermine our communion with God and draw us into habits that oppose the sanctity and dignity of our bodies and souls.

Constantly indulging in sense gratification primes the soul for temptation, especially in matters of sexual purity. When we habitually engage in activities that flood the senses—such as endless scrolling on social media, binge-watching shows, or continually seeking novel forms of entertainment—we train ourselves to seek immediate pleasure without discipline or restraint. Social media, for instance, exposes us to carefully curated images that often promote superficial beauty, wealth, and fame, subtly embedding lustful desires and envious thoughts within us. Each indulgence weakens our resistance to further temptation, gradually making us more vulnerable to sexual sin. This lack of moderation distorts our perception of true fulfillment, as we become conditioned to chase fleeting pleasures rather than cultivating virtue and self-control. These habits are ultimately insidious because they deepen our dependency on momentary gratifications, drawing us away from God and from a pure, ordered life aligned with His will.

CULTIVATING A LIFE OF PURITY

The path to overcoming concupiscence is often arduous in the beginning, as the pull of past habits and inclinations can seem relentless. Yet, with perseverance in God's grace, consistent participation in the sacraments, and a firm pursuit of virtue, this struggle gradually becomes lighter. As we grow in holiness, the temptations that once felt overpowering begin to lose their grip, and purity of heart becomes more natural. Reaching this stage brings a profound freedom; while remnants of concupiscence may still occasionally arise, they are far easier to resist. In this newfound strength, we taste the peace and clarity that come with true mastery over the self, experiencing a closeness to God that transforms our lives and draws us ever nearer to the sanctity for which we were created.

CHOOSING HOLINESS OVER COMPROMISE: A CALL TO PURITY IN RELATIONSHIPS

If you find yourself in a relationship with someone you are not married to, and sin has already entered your union, it is crucial to examine your path. If there is no intention of marriage, then there is no need to justify ending the relationship. You are not called to risk your eternal soul for the sake of pleasing another person; you owe them no explanation that leads you back into sin. Letting go of this relationship is a necessary step toward honoring God, who calls you to purity and holiness.

However, if marriage is indeed your goal, then approach your partner with honesty: express the need to repent together, to wait until marriage, and to honor God by rejecting contraception. A truly committed partner will understand and respect this decision, embracing the path of holiness with you. But if they do not respect this call to purity, then it is time to part ways. You are called to a life that leads to God, and no relationship is worth sacrificing your soul. Seek only those who will walk beside you in faith, lifting you closer to Christ and supporting your journey to eternal life.

PRACTICAL STEPS FOR MAINTAINING PURITY AND RESISTING TEMPTATION

1. Develop a strong prayer life by praying the Morning Offering, the Rosary, the Our Father, and the Night Prayer daily.
2. Frequent confession strengthens resolve, cleanses the soul of sin, and provides grace to resist future temptations.
3. Receive the Eucharist in a state of grace to fortify yourself spiritually, uniting with Christ and increasing strength against temptation.
4. Spend time in Eucharistic Adoration, which offers grace, peace, and an increased ability to resist temptations.
5. When a lustful thought arises, do not dwell on it. Redirect your mind to something positive, such as a prayer or an act of gratitude.
6. Shift your focus immediately if a tempting thought arises to avoid forming an attachment. Replace such thoughts with prayer or focus on a productive task.
7. Avoid excessive time on social media or entertainment platforms that may expose you to lustful content.
8. Choose wholesome shows, movies, and music that align with virtue. Avoid media with sexually explicit content or messages that normalize impurity.
9. Use internet filters or accountability software to block or monitor inappropriate content.
10. Avoid places, situations, or people that might lead you into sexual temptation.
11. When needed, have an accountability partner for support in situations of temptation or to help avoid risky scenarios.
12. Avoid being alone in moments when you are likely to feel tempted. Engage in wholesome activities with others instead.

13. Seek guidance from a trusted mentor to help navigate challenges, as this can be a source of strength.
14. Engage in acts of kindness and charity. Filling your life with positive actions reduces the likelihood of turning to sin.
15. Practice small acts of self-denial daily, such as fasting or delaying gratification. These help strengthen willpower.
16. Recognize the need for God's help in overcoming temptation and avoid pride by acknowledging weaknesses.
17. Surround yourself with friends who value chastity and virtue.
18. Dress and conduct yourself with respect for your own dignity and the dignity of others, which can help reduce temptations for yourself and those around you.
19. Understand the teachings on chastity, the sacredness of marriage, and the purpose of sexuality to deepen your conviction to live them out.
20. Study the lives of saints who struggled with or championed purity, as their examples can be inspiring and motivating.
21. If a lustful image or thought appears, acknowledge it and then shift your attention within three seconds to break its hold on your mind.
22. Identify specific prayers, thoughts, or physical actions (like leaving a room or stepping outside) that help you in moments of temptation.
23. When tempted, immediately start a productive task that requires focus, helping to redirect your attention.
24. If you fall, turn back to God immediately with repentance. Do not let shame or guilt prevent you from seeking reconciliation.
25. Regularly thank God for His mercy, recognizing that He provides grace for every struggle and always invites you to return to Him.

Conclusion

The exploration of the transformation of human nature after original sin underscores the far-reaching impact of Adam and Eve's disobedience on humanity. The loss of original holiness and justice, as articulated by the Council of Trent and St. Robert Bellarmine, set the stage for the enduring struggle with sin and mortality that characterizes human existence. This doctrinal understanding emphasizes the indispensable role of Jesus Christ's redemptive sacrifice in restoring divine grace and opening the way to eternal life. Through the sacrament of baptism, believers are afforded the grace to become friends and heirs of God, highlighting the profound hope and promise of ultimate restoration and eternal union with the divine.

"The Effects of Original Sin: Altered Human Nature" underscores the significant impact of Adam and Eve's disobedience, which transformed human nature from its original state of justice and holiness to one of injustice and unholiness. This transformation, known as concupiscence, represents a profound inclination toward sin and an attraction to pleasure that persists even after baptism. This inherited weakness manifests as an internal struggle, often leading to morally wrong desires and actions. Recognizing concupiscence is essential for understanding the human condition and the need for divine grace, self-discipline, and moral vigilance to resist sinful inclinations. Through this understanding, individuals can better navigate the challenges posed by this altered nature and strive for spiritual strength and redemption.

The doctrine of original sin elucidates the profound impact of Adam and Eve's disobedience on human nature and existence. Their transgression not only brought about spiritual and physical death but also disrupted the harmonious relationships they once enjoyed with God, each other, and creation. This act of rebellion, rooted in pride and the desire for autonomy, introduced a distorted moral order and a persistent inclination toward sin. Consequently, humanity now grapples with a fallen nature, marked by a tendency toward moral failings and a disrupted communion with the divine. The necessity of baptism, even for infants, underscores the Church's recognition of the pervasive stain of original sin and the need for divine grace to restore our relationship with God. Ultimately, the story of original sin serves as a cautionary tale about the dangers of deviating from God's established moral order and the profound consequences that follow from such disobedience.

Original sin, stemming from Adam's transgression, represents a profound alteration of human nature, casting a shadow over all of humanity. According to the Council of Trent, the only remedy for this inherited corruption is the sacrifice of Jesus Christ. This passage underscores the unique and indispensable role of Christ's redemptive act in reconciling humanity with God. By His blood, Christ offers not only atonement for sin but also the means to restore humanity to its original state of justice and holiness. This divine intervention is essential, as human efforts alone cannot address the deep-seated effects of original sin. The passage explores the necessity of Christ's sacrifice, the limitations of human nature in overcoming sin, and the transformative power of divine grace through the sacraments, highlighting the enduring need for Christ's redemptive work in the life of every believer.

In summary, the theological rationale for baptizing infants is deeply rooted in the understanding of original sin as inherited from Adam. Despite the baptism of the parents, the necessity of infant baptism is affirmed by Church doctrine to cleanse the child of this inherited defect. Through baptism, infants are freed from the stain of original sin, becoming new creations in Christ and entering into a state of grace. This sacrament is not merely symbolic but a vital and efficacious means of grace, crucial for ensuring that every soul is prepared to enter the Kingdom of Heaven. The Church's teachings, supported by early theologians and Councils, underscore the indispensable role of baptism in the spiritual life, reinforcing its significance as a foundational act of faith and grace.

In conclusion, while baptism effectively removes the guilt of original sin and grants a restored relationship with God, it does not eliminate the ongoing struggle with concupiscence or the possibility of personal sin. This struggle underscores the necessity of continued vigilance and adherence to the sacramental economy of the Church. The Protestant doctrine of sola fide fails to fully address the reality of post-baptismal sin, as it often overlooks the essential role of the sacraments in maintaining and restoring grace. The Catholic understanding emphasizes that, despite the initial grace of baptism, the sacrament of reconciliation remains crucial for addressing serious sin and preserving the integrity of one's relationship with God. By engaging in the Church's sacramental life, believers receive the grace and support necessary to navigate the ongoing challenges of sin and remain steadfast in their commitment to living according to God's will.

Bibliography

"The object of anger is good or evil, because it seeks to inflict harm in response to perceived injustice." Summa Theologica. Translated by Fathers of the English Dominican Province, Second and Revised Edition, 1920, New Advent,

https://www.newadvent.org/summa/4048.htm.

Anselm (saint). Why God Became Man. Magi Publications, 1969.

Augustine, and Aeterna Press. A Treatise on the Grace of Christ and on Original Sin. Aeterna Press.

Bellarmine, Robert, et al. Doctrina Christiana: The Timeless Catechism of St. Robert Bellarmine. Lulu.com, 28 Sept. 2016.

Benedict, Pope. In the Beginning--: A Catholic Understanding of the Story of Creation and the Fall. Grand Rapids, Mich., W.B. Eerdmans Pub. Co, 1995.

Catholic Church. (2019). Catechism of the Catholic Church. Vatican City, LibreriaEditriceVaticana; Washington, D.C.

Coffin, P. (2018). The contraception deception: Catholic teaching on birth control. Emmaus
Road Publishing

Day 55: The Fall of the Angels — The Catechism in a Year (with Fr. Mike Schmitz)
https://www.youtube.com/watch?v=QiJL024zpmc

Henri Rondet, Original Sin: The Patristic and Theological Background. Saint Pauls/Alba House, 1 Jan. 1972.

Maria, Alfonso, and John Thomas Mullock. The History of Heresies, and Their Refutation, Or, the Triumph of the Church; Volume 1. Legare Street Press.

Of Hippo, Augustine,. City of God. Translated by Marcus Dods, Digireads.com Publishing, 2017.

Peter Lombard, Sentences, Volume 2, trans. Guilio Silano, (Toronto: Pontifical Institute of Mediaeval Studies, 2007).

Pope Paul VI. (1968, July 25). Humanae Vitae. Www.vatican.va. https://www.vatican.va/content/paul-vi/en/encyclicals/documents/hf_p vi_enc_25071968_humanae-vitae.html

The Canons and Decrees of the Council of Trent. Translated by H.J. Schroeder, TAN Books and Publishers, 1978.

Thomas Aquinas. SummaTheologiae: Prima SecundaePartis. Translated by the Fathers of the English Dominican Province, Aquinas Institute, Green Bay, WI.

University of Notre Dame McGrath Institute for Church Life. (n.d.). Foundations of Catholic Belief. Unit 4: Salvation in Jesus Christ, Section "Sin and Its Effects" (CCC, 355-421 and 2331-2347). Retrieved from mcgrath.nd.edu.

Explore More from Sanctus Virtue Publishing
Championing Classical Virtue and Timeless Wisdom

How Heretics Dismantled the Medieval Catholic Patriarchal Family Unit to Usher in Modern Secularism: Insights from the Reformation and French Revolution on the Shift from Christendom to Secularism

By Christopher Ross

ISBN: 979-8-9916647-4-5

Explores how heretical movements and pivotal events like the Reformation and the French Revolution dismantled the medieval Catholic patriarchal family unit, reshaping marriage, family, and societal structures to pave the way for modern secularism, and redefining the moral and legal landscapes we navigate today.

***

The French Revolution of 1789: Its War on the Classical Pillars of Western Society and the Rise of Secularism: Analysis of the Revolution's Attack on the Church, Monarchy, Tradition, and Patriarchy

By Christopher Ross

ISBN: 979-8991664707

Uncover the revolutionary upheavals that dismantled Western society's traditional foundations and led to the rise of secularism.

***

Catholic vs. Protestant Doctrine: Defending the Faith Against the Protestant Reformation's Heresies: A Catholic Apologetic Analysis of Sola Scriptura, Sola Fide, Purgatory, and Papal Infallibility

By Christopher Ross

ISBN: 979-8-9916647-1-4

An in-depth defense of Catholic doctrine, responding to the key Protestant reformations and providing insights into essential theological debates.

***

The Divine Balance: Authority, Governance, and Spiritual Supremacy in Traditional Christendom: Exploring the Interplay of Secular and Spiritual Powers from the Medieval Era to Modern America

By Christopher Ross

ISBN: 979-8-9916647-3-8

Examine the historical balance between secular authority and spiritual supremacy, and how this dynamic has evolved throughout Christendom.

www.ingramcontent.com/pod-product-compliance
Lightning Source LLC
Chambersburg PA
CBHW060848050426
42453CB00008B/884